CW01304833

Control Your Emotions:
Gain Balance, Resilience, and Calm; Find Freedom from Stress, Anxiety, and Negativity

By Patrick King
Social Interaction and Conversation Coach at
www.PatrickKingConsulting.com

Table of Contents

Chapter 1. Our Volatile Emotions
Emotional Origins
The Purpose of Emotions

Chapter 2. Emotional Triggers
The Nature of Triggers
Emotional *Needs*
The Emotional Spectrum

Chapter 3. Recognize, Respond, and Regulate
A Regulation Framework
Distress Tolerance

Chapter 4. Cutting the Cycle
The ABC Loop
Emotional Dashboarding
Healthy Self-Talk

Chapter 5. The Emotional Immune System
Mind Games
The Self-Esteem Cycle

Chapter 6. Philosophical Perspective
Detachment
Reinterpret Neutrality

Chapter 7. Preventative Care
Be Grateful and Savor
Write It Out
Stay in the Present
Boundary Defense

Summary Guide

Chapter 1. Our Volatile Emotions

Though I wasn't the best student in school, I was able to develop a close friendship with my high school English teacher, Mr. Locke.

I'm not sure why he took an interest in me, but I suppose a convenient narrative is that he's the reason I ended up as a writer, and I have him to thank for all of it. Unfortunately, that would be false to say, as it's not remotely what we talked about most of the time.

Throughout the whole year, it was enlightening to ask him about the books we were reading for class and what he *actually* thought about them. *The Adventures of Tom Sawyer*? Overrated. *The Great Gatsby*? His favorite of all time. *Of Mice and Men*? He preferred the movie.

However, things got really interesting when the end of the year drew close, and he started to open up about the people in my class—my peers. Of course, this was a dream come true for me: an adult willing to gossip with me about my fellow students. Looking back, it was wildly inappropriate for Mr. Locke to engage in such topics with me, but it's not like the teachers weren't doing it amongst themselves, anyway.

He let me in on a little secret of his: whenever he had to give negative feedback, he would always make sure to try to build up the individual student a couple of days before. He would do this to make sure their self-esteem, at least in the realm of his class, was sufficiently high, such that his negative feedback wouldn't have as big of an impact. He wanted students to not take things so personally and be able to separate his comments on their work from them as a person. Too many students in the past had received his feedback in less than ideal ways. He wanted them to hear, "This paper could use work," not "*You* need work."

My teenage mind was blown away, and I told him that he was so clever to use "Jedi mind tricks" on his students. He told me there were a few students he would do this on more than others because he felt they had low self-esteem or he knew they were being bullied outside of his class. My adult mind still admires him and thinks that he had tremendous insight into how people worked—especially future adults that were still figuring themselves out and who had fragile egos. It wasn't until much later that I realized he was helping students gain emotional resilience through raising their self-esteem.

Self-esteem is an essential component of emotional resilience and is often deemed *the immune system of emotions*. When it's high, you can handle what's thrown your way, and when it's low, you are more likely to collapse under scrutiny. Mr. Locke had somehow dialed into that and instilled that into his students.

Emotional resilience is a trait that is like the background music in a movie. When it's there, you don't notice it and it seems that scenes just fit together without a hitch. However, if it's missing, suddenly words are taken the wrong way, everything feels wrong, and the scene falls apart. In other words, you notice it when you need it, but not when you don't.

Therein lies the conundrum of resilience, emotional stability, and strength in the face of tragedy and despair—how do you get it before you need it, and how do you know if you don't have it? The ugly truth is that none of us are naturally born with it. Some of us are put into nasty situations where we develop coping mechanisms for strength, but that doesn't mean you are resilient. It just means the dam hasn't broken yet. And what will you do when the dam breaks?

It can be a scary realization or an empowering one—*I've gotten this far without being truly resilient? Good things are ahead. It's all downhill from here.*

The hope for this book is to arm you, whoever you are and whatever you may or may not have suffered, with tools and techniques to persevere and thrive. Emotional resilience is one of those rare qualities that cause a drastic shift in how you see the world. More importantly, it allows you to see *you* and gain better self-awareness of your thought patterns and behaviors. First understanding and then being able to harness and master your emotions gives you a lens of safety and control over the world, which gives you the feeling of being able to do anything.

Emotions are a major part of our existence and our identity as humans. Yet we don't often take a moment to think about where they come from, what they mean, why we feel certain ways, and how emotion actually affects us.

Why did I cry at that movie?
Because it was sad.
But why did I cry?

Because that's what you do when you're sad.
But… why?

We just accept that we are affected and don't take the time to think about how to strengthen or regulate certain emotions for greater well-being. Unfortunately, it's this lack of attention that leads precisely to a lack of resilience. If you don't understand the forces at work inside your brain, you can only fall prey to them, with no hope of regulating or even combating them. As such, we are completely at the whims of our emotional brain.

Mastering and conquering our emotional brains requires a bit of knowledge and background into what you are going to be battling. How do emotions function, what is their role, and why are they capable of completely dictating our lives?

Emotional Origins

What makes us feel emotions? How do we know and understand what we feel and *why* we feel it? If you were to ask 100 people to answer those questions, you would probably get 100 answers. Ultimately, it boils down to a study in neuroscience, but we will first explore two standard theories to explain the emotions that color our lives.

The first theory is called the *cognitive appraisal theory*, put forth by Swiss psychologist Klaus Scherer.

This theory states that emotions are judgments about the extent that a current situation meets your expectations and goals, no matter how you define them. Happiness is felt because it is an evaluation that your expectations are being met or even exceeded. If you win the lottery, you feel happiness because it solves your financial needs and likely exceeds your expectations. If you're asked out on a date, you feel happiness because it holds the promise of satisfying your romantic needs. In the same way, when you feel sadness, it is an evaluation that your goals are not being met or fall below expectations, and anger might be the feeling that is aimed at whatever is blocking your goals.

Here, emotions are an instinctual reaction to objects or situations that relate to your expectations and goals. Often our goals are not clearly defined, as they can be both subconscious and conscious. You may not be able to say exactly why you're happy or disappointed at times—this theory sheds light on the fact that you subconsciously held some type of expectation that was or was not met.

If you are unemployed and presented with a job offer, you will feel happiness because you see it as a way to solve your financial worries. Alternatively, if you lose your job, you are saddened because you lose your financial stability. Your emotions are tied to how your status quo changes—another way we hold expectations we don't realize. In some cases, it may have little to do with the situation itself; maybe you've always hated your job and have always wanted to leave it. But when you're faced with the unexpected loss, you are saddened because it represents the loss of stability and your future career.

The cognitive appraisal theory speaks to your perception of how well a situation meets your goals and expectations, so your emotions will be a reflection of that. Understanding this theory means that you can better evaluate your emotions by always determining what they are oriented toward. It essentially states that your emotions require something to revolve around.

This could seem overly simplistic, and indeed, it's mostly useful for background for other, more-involved theories of emotion. It might serve as a good rule of thumb, however, and help you realize if you are holding subconscious expectations one way or another.

The second explanation of the nature of emotions is that they are purely an interpretation of the body's signals.

Psychologists William James and Carl Lange proposed that emotions are just the perceptions of change in the physiology of your body—for example, changes in heart rate, breathing, perspiration, and hormone levels. This theory argues that emotions such as happiness are merely a physiological perception instead of a judgment as the previous theory states. Other emotions like sadness and anger are also mental reactions to different kinds of biological functions.

According to James and Lange, your body's state will change first as a reaction to an external stimulus, which will spur you to associate an emotion with it. For example, imagine you are about to perform a speech in front of a group of people and think of your body's reaction beforehand. You might feel your heart pumping faster or your breathing increasing slightly. Your mind will associate the combination of these physical reactions with a feeling of nervousness.

There is undoubtedly a connection between emotions and physiological changes. However, the problem with this account is that bodily states are not nearly as fine-tuned or diverse as the many different kinds of emotions. Returning to the previous example, your heart pumping and increased breathing may also be interpreted as a feeling of excitement because of the close physiological similarities. This is the problem with associating emotions with physical reactions, because you often have more emotions than reactions, and many biological responses are too similar to differentiate.

Understanding that emotions may be tied to your physical reactions means you may be able to convince yourself of alternative emotions. Imagine you are about to partake in some public speaking. Telling yourself that you are excited instead of nervous, considering the similarity in bodily reactions, may help you better face the task ahead of you. It can be quite beneficial to perceive negative physiological signs and use them for positive purposes.

Neither of these theories tell the entire story; one is focused on emotions as thoughts, and the other is focused on emotions as physiology. In truth, they work hand in hand.

Emotions, in the most general definition, are a neural impulse that moves you to act. They are something the brain commands to achieve a better existence, one that has evolved over time to help us survive and meet certain needs.

Psychologist Linda Davidoff defines emotion as a feeling that is expressed through physiological functions such as facial expressions, heartbeat, and certain behavior such as aggression, crying, or covering the face with hands. According to her, emotions are a result of changes in the brain, where neurochemicals such as dopamine, noradrenaline, and serotonin increase or lower the brain's activity level according to what is more beneficial in the circumstances.

For example, the human emotion of love is proposed to have evolved from circuits in the brain that were stimulated and designed for the care, feeding, and grooming of offspring. Having offspring around eventually cemented these pathways and associated it with positive, nurturing behavior.

Emotion makes us act a certain way based on the stimuli that we have processed and is the interpretation of a series of physical changes. When you are in a situation where your palms begin to sweat, your heartbeat increases, and you are actively searching your surroundings, your body will do these physical things without much thought. They are reactive. But your mind will subsequently interpret the combination of these behavioral changes with a feeling of fear. First you have the stimuli, then the physical reactions, and then the psychological reaction—the emotion—that comes after.

It's important to note that often the brain is wrong, and the brain's concept of "beneficial" is not always compatible with the modern age.

When neurologists deeply explored the brain, they discovered that depression, love, kindness, aggression, abstract thinking, judgment, patience, instincts, and memories all have specific biochemical causes and even physical locations. Because all of these feelings, emotions, and characteristics have foundations in the brain, this means that they can all be radically affected by brain damage and brain surgery.

One of the most famous examples of brain structure altering emotions and personality is the curious case of Phineas Gage. In 1848, a work explosion led to a metal pole going straight through Gage's skull. Despite the injury, he survived, albeit with an enormous hole in his skull and with a sizable part of his brain missing for the rest of his life. The damage to his frontal lobes caused a radical change in his personality and character. Prior to the accident, he was conscientious, upright, and respected. After the accident, he was suddenly abusive, profane, irritable, and irresponsible. He was simply a different person, unrecognizable to family and friends.

There was no other possible conclusion other than the areas that were destroyed regulated certain parts of the personality and certain emotions. Later, neurologists explained this more precisely, in that the brain's frontal lobes are associated with moderating impulsive behavior, setting goals, and other abstract areas of thought. Those around him described him as having become fitful, irreverent, prone to the "grossest profanity which was not previously his custom," and "a child in his intellectual capacity" but with "the animal passions of a strong man."

Gage's case was one of the first true revelations that proved that emotions originated from a biological source and were a direct result of the brain, instead of being associated with the soul, heart, or simple expectations.

Modern research indicates that during events, the sensory information that you pick up is transmitted to the thalamus, the relay center of the brain, before being transferred to the amygdala and the prefrontal cortex. The amygdala instantly processes the information and sends signals so that hormones are released that activate the autonomic nervous system. Meanwhile, the prefrontal cortex slowly processes the sensory information from the thalamus in the background, a slower system overall.

The amygdala causes a person's instantaneous response to an emotion-evoking event. There is no thought in this; it is pure instinct. The brain has evolved to have two different tracks of stimuli-processing: one quick and one slower. The quicker one is designed for protection and survival: when the amygdala thinks there is a threat that must be acted upon immediately in one way or another. Alternatively, the prefrontal cortex is responsible for gradual processing, which allows someone to evaluate the emotion-evoking event and even regulate their emotions surrounding it.

This fast and slow reaction is something that can be seen in everyday life and is much simpler when seen firsthand. If there is a sound in the middle of the night that wakes you, you will instantly be alert and ready for action, even if you've had little sleep and your whole body is exhausted. This is an instinctual reaction to a threat so that you have chances at survival. This is something that can easily be traced back as a result of evolution. If you are slow to respond to threats, you will not be able to survive.

On the other hand, the slow processing of external stimuli in the prefrontal cortex is for less-instinctual emotions. Something like love takes longer to process because of the number of contributing factors. It is not instinctual to feel love when presented with an event or situation. It takes a bit longer and more processing of the overall situation.

So what are emotions? We've discovered that they are part biological and part based on evaluating the world around us. But they are far more than that, as any romantic comedy will show you. Perhaps the best and most helpful way to conceive of emotions is this: they depend on your unique brain chemistry, your circumstances and status quo, your expectations, and your entire life of experiences that inform everything prior.

The Purpose of Emotions

The purpose of emotions really stems from that track of processing that goes directly to the amygdala for instant action.

They are one of the most important indicators of what will keep us alive and happy by letting us know what we should avoid and what we should pursue. Think of emotions as the mental version of your sense of taste. You will avoid foods that don't taste good, such as rotten fruit, because they are likely to be bad for you, and you will actively eat what tastes good to you because they are likely to be good for your health and survival—though not your waistline. Of course, this is why fat tastes amazing and why feces have a foul smell.

Emotions go a level further than helping you avoid rotten fruit. They help you avoid dangerous situations, psychological damage, and less-subtle dangers that are just as fatal.

Emotions lead to the well-being and ultimate survival of both individuals and groups by providing a quick and automated reaction to certain events and circumstances. This is so that we can avoid danger and take advantage of opportunities. This can be seen in both animals and humans. However, unlike animals, human emotions often clash with socially and culturally acquired conventions and rules. In this case, these automated responses may actually be disruptive and less adaptive than consciously deliberated responses. Tears of sadness may have garnered sympathy, but it can also denote weakness and a moment where someone's defenses are down.

Emotion is beneficial because it causes an organism to carry out certain preset behaviors that have been adapted over time to lead to the best outcome. In most cases of emotion, our movements lead to developing an intense focus on the object that triggered the emotion, something that focuses all our attention. This can be seen in behaviors like freezing in place, fleeing from a threat, or nurturing our young. All these actions are caused directly because of our reactions to specific emotions. If it's not positive focus, it's negative, paranoid fixation. They both assist survival.

An example of this is when a herd of deer is grazing, and even if only one of them hears the slightest noise, the entire herd looks up and concentrates very specifically on its surroundings and is able to identify and focus on a nearby lion before fleeing. A human example might be when a parent hears their child scream from across a room. They are immediately focused on nothing but their child and develop tunnel vision until they find out what's wrong. This happens because we are inclined to have a much greater focus on the object that causes whatever emotion we are feeling.

Along with pure survival instinct, emotions also serve to alert us to threats based on our past experiences. We all develop "emotional programs" that we adopt in situations that warrant emotion. For example, we have had to learn how and whom we can trust, how to cope with failure, and how to react to death. These all come with behaviors that we have had to learn over time so that we know how to act in certain emotional situations.

Based on the above, the purpose of emotions is to first detect evolutionary survival cues, then trigger reactions that have worked in the past and that we have deemed as good solutions to those problems. It is a continuous commentary on how we, and others around us, see the meaning of things. Some emotions are automatically signaled because we have such an immediate and quick reaction to them. Other emotions, such as jealousy or guilt, can be harder to identify and consciously react to. In either case, emotions help us because we are able to see what they are pointing an arrow at.

You may have noticed that since emotion has the convenient purpose of keeping us alive, it tends to have a negative bias. Negative emotions are more noticeable to us because attending to negative events is often more important to our survival than dealing with positive events. The worst outcome when you delay a reaction to a positive event—for example, a birthday, a promotion, or a wedding—is that you celebrate a little later than you normally would have. However, with a negative event, there are much worse things that can happen if our reactions are delayed. It seems quite appropriate that we focus on dealing with negative things first, as they have the power to kill us, whereas positive events merely enhance our well-being.

There is an infinite number of ways that situations can take a turn for the worse rather than taking a turn for the better. The night before a big event, we are most often thinking about every single thing that could go wrong, not everything that could go right. If any of these possibilities actually occur, you need to deal with them, so it's better that you imagine them and aren't caught off guard. Appropriately, negative emotions take up more mental bandwidth. Avoiding death is simply more important than eating cake.

There is no shame in feeling your emotions; we simply want to do so in an appropriate and healthy manner.

In a 2012 study, psychotherapist Eric L. Garland of Florida State University gathered 58 adults in treatment for alcohol dependence and measured their responses to stress based on heart rate when exposing them to alcohol-related cues. The results found that those who restrained their thinking and suppressed their emotions more had much stronger stress responses to the cues than those who suppressed less frequently.

Even if you think you have successfully bypassed a stressor, there is no guarantee that your subconscious has also stopped dwelling on it. In 2011, psychologist

Richard A. Bryant of the University of New South Wales in Sydney conducted a study where half the participants were told to suppress an unwanted thought prior to sleep. Those who tried to suppress their thoughts reported that they dreamed about it more, a phenomenon called *dream rebound*.

Both of these studies demonstrate that emotional suppression not only doesn't work, but can also be immensely harmful. It can cause you to fixate more on what you are avoiding and can be detrimental to your physical health. As if this wasn't evidence enough, another study in the United States by experts at the Harvard School of Public Health and the University of Rochester showed that those who fail to say or express how they feel increased their risk of premature death from all causes by about 35%. When researchers evaluated specific causes of death, they uncovered that the risks increased by 47% for heart disease and 70% for cancer.

Death rates are highest among those most likely to bottle up their emotion rather than express it to others and let them know how they feel.

Emotions are at the center of almost all that we do and who we are. And yet we don't have to be held hostage by them. We must strike a fine balance between fully feeling them, not suppressing them, and regulating them.

Takeaways:

- Our emotions have enormous power over us. Sometimes this is good, and other times, it makes us feel completely out of control. This is bad. But there is good reason for this type of power—you can view emotions as a type of warning signal that has evolved alongside humans to keep us alive and healthy. In the absence of higher critical thinking, emotions taught us about the world and how to regard it. This is also the reason that negative emotions can make us spiral out of control so quickly.

- These types of dangers aren't present anymore in our modern lives, and our task now is less survival and more controlling and harnessing our emotions. The extent to which we do this can wholly determine how our lives go. In no way is this suggesting that emotional suppression is the key to happiness. In fact, emotional suppression is linked to poor health outcomes, so we must simply find the fine line of healthy emotional expression and reaction.

Chapter 2. Emotional Triggers

We've all heard it and we've all felt it: a small provocation that can send our emotions spiraling in a direction that we didn't anticipate and that objectively shouldn't have any impact whatsoever.

This could be that one song that reminds you of something extremely traumatic or maybe that one person you don't see often enough, but when you do, your emotions are out of your control. It could even be mentioning a single word, such as a name or the word "fat," that is the tip of the iceberg in terms of what it represents to you.

These are *emotional triggers*: things that elicit an immediate emotional response. There are positive ones and negative ones, but we don't need help with positive ones. Some can lead to positive emotions, like discovering an item from your childhood that you immediately associate with happiness or love. It boils down to something you have special sensitivity to, and it can impact you for the entire day or even week. With only a few words, you are feeling entirely off-center and fall into a pit of anxiety, depression, guilt, or shame.

Why are we so deeply affected by something that we rationally know should not affect us as badly as it does? Can't we be logical creatures that aren't ruled by our emotions?

Yes and no. We have emotional triggers because we have lived, struggled, and come of age. No matter how lucky you have been in life, you have had moments of hardship and trauma you never want to experience again. Things that happen in the past, especially when we were children, are often ingrained deep into our minds. We may not have been able to deal with the pain or suffering or embarrassment that we felt when we were younger, so we suppress it—in fact, that's the logical part. We work hard to avoid, deny, or ignore things to keep our days pain- and worry-free. And years later, when we are adults, reminders of our pain can bring those feelings screaming back. It's not productive to go completely down the Sigmund Freud route and assume that all of your adult pains are the result of childhood traumas, but we can say that our triggers and causes of pain from which we want peace and escape are rooted somewhere in the past.

And within the past, there is usually a story; sometimes it isn't something you can pinpoint but a variety of events that lead to a painful idea overall. There is nothing wrong with you if a painful memory triggers pain; it just means you're human. It doesn't mean you're weak or mentally ill, because everyone does the same. It's just a feeling that we have because of what something may lead you to think or what something may represent to you. For instance, the pain of being constantly berated and ridiculed for being overweight as a child is something you can easily imagine to cause multiple emotional triggers in adulthood. You may be extremely sensitive about your weight, or you might have developed eating disorders to cope with those feelings of inadequacy. You might feel an overwhelming need to exercise for hours a day, or you might still have a terrible body image and see an obese person in the mirror.

After you are triggered, how do you act when you suddenly experience great pain? You retreat into whatever habits or defense mechanisms you've developed over the years. For some, this will be physically withdrawing, while for others, it means a complete mental breakdown into a state of hysteria. The worst reactions will prevent you from living your life as you want, and this is the real downside to feeling our emotions fully.

The word *trigger* is an important point here. The idea of an emotional trigger is that it is something that occurs automatically. One of the goals of this book is to move away from this automatic, involuntary path and onto a more conscious path. By learning how to identify your emotional triggers, you can start to seize control of your compulsions and respond rather than react. Once you start becoming aware of these triggers, you can begin to monitor them and realize that you can intervene in the period of time between the trigger and your response. This intervention is the key to changing the outcome of the situation and trying to get a more desirable result.

Emotional triggers often lie behind some of our worst behaviors. If you think about negative behaviors that seem automatic or out of your control, then you may just be unaware of the emotional trigger that caused it. Triggers are very personal. Different things trigger different people, and so a trigger for you may not affect another person at all.

The emotional intensity that is felt by a trigger is of a similar intensity as the initial trauma itself, which perfectly explains why anyone would want to avoid it. These triggers can be activated by any of the five senses: sight, sound, smell, touch, and taste.

When looking to better respond to your triggers, you need to identify the trigger itself first. The external stimuli may appear to be innocent, but it could be a trigger simply because of what it represents to you. It may have nothing to do with the words that someone said to you and more to do with the links you make in your mind.

Perhaps a comment is made about you never attending college. This is a plain fact, but it may also make you think about other things you never had the chance to do or things that you missed out on. It might make you feel small and lesser than the people around you. Does this comment mean that you are dumber than the people around you? Is everyone in on the joke except you? How dare they imply that traditional higher education is the only way to be a respectable member of society.

A single sentence has the power to unlock all of these wayward thoughts. As a trigger, sometimes you can't help but follow this train of negativity. The following thoughts had nothing to do with the initial trigger, but you were led there regardless.

It is the *story* of the trigger that is important, no matter how significant. Finding the story behind the trigger is key to solving it and changing your responses.

The Nature of Triggers

For our purposes, we will think about triggers as purely external; there is an external event that gives rise to an internal reaction. External triggers might be benign or harmful by themselves, but remember, they aren't necessarily related to why you might experience an emotional breakdown. Examples of external triggers include the following:

- being rejected or abandoned
- helplessness in painful situations
- being ignored
- being misunderstood
- when someone is angry at you
- being mocked
- being treated unequally
- when someone doesn't make time for you
- being vulnerable or exposed
- when someone shows disapproval
- being blamed or shamed
- being judged
- when someone isn't happy to see you
- when someone is trying to control you

None of these are rare in everyday life. In fact, someone might not actually be rejecting you, but it's what you will perceive if it is a trigger for you. For some, they are just the tip of the emotional iceberg and are related to much deeper-rooted pains and wounds. This is why people's emotions may escalate very quickly in response to a trigger. In other words, the former list of triggers is a direct reminder of negative associations involving the following list:

- acceptance
- respect
- being understood
- being in control
- attention
- being needed or liked
- being treated fairly
- being included
- predictability
- safety
- insecurity
- pride
- lack of confidence
- love

There are repeated and overlapping themes. Once these emotions are triggered, the typical response is certainly not to calmly address it, but rather intellectualize it out of existence or lash out in an attempt to cope. Both tend to lead to self-destructive behavior, and this also means the next time you face the same emotional trigger, it may even have a worse effect on you.

The coping mechanisms that we develop as a result can vary. We may create interpersonal conflict, act in a passive or aggressive manner, or stop communicating at all. The problem with these negative coping mechanisms is that over time they will become patterns that produce further emotional stress, drain our energy, and influence our lives and our work. You'll begin with distress about your trigger; then the distress will compound as you notice the effects of your negative coping mechanisms and how much you want to stop your behavior patterns. These self-destructive habits may include the following:

- lashing out at people
- becoming needy and attention-seeking
- becoming a people-pleaser and ignoring your own needs
- completely withdrawing from others
- deflecting blame onto others
- becoming addicted to soothing behavior, such as food, alcohol, sex, drugs, shopping, and so on

The whole situation, from trigger to coping mechanism, is doomed from the start because of all the negativity that surrounds it.

Imagine you are at work and are asked to do a certain task, such as handing in a report or something similar that your employer expects and trusts you to complete. You do as you're told, but his feedback is not ideal. Though you may have put a lot of time into the project, he is unsatisfied and finishes off by saying he is disappointed.

Those words could be the trigger for you: the idea of disappointment. It isn't so much that you have to fix the report—that's something that will only take an hour or two. It's the fact that you let someone down. Maybe you can relate that to your own childhood and a situation where your parents depended on you but, in the end, weren't able to rely on you after all. The weight of a parent's disapproval is something that is hard to accept, even as an adult, but especially as a child. Logically, you know you aren't a child any longer and the situation is different, but triggers aren't rational. Someone that is in a semi-paternal role to you, your supervisor, has given you a negative evaluation, and that brings feelings of inadequacy flooding back.

From there you become withdrawn and turn away from everyone else, especially those who care about you. Being alone only allows the negativity to fester and build further, and you begin to wonder if people hate you. Negative thoughts sustain themselves by adding more negativity to the fire, and you will berate yourself even if you're not sure why you feel so badly. Subconsciously, the story you've told yourself from childhood is in full effect. Feelings of insecurity, anger, remorse, or guilt will make themselves felt as well. You are feeding into a constant cycle where every rejection or disappointment will lead you to replicate this behavior, and this compounds as you feel bad about the behavior itself. Is there even an exit for this ride, or are you doomed to stay in the cycle?

Does this sound familiar? You can easily recognize this as self-destructive behavior, but it's not so easy to stop the freight train when you're in the heat of the moment. This is a classic example of an external trigger (the disappointing comment from your supervisor) that digs deep into your psyche and conjures up something that is only tangentially related (the disappointment from your childhood). This isn't a sequence you can stop without deeper self-understanding.

Emotional *Needs*

Specifically, we must understand what emotional need is being exposed, or poked, when we encounter an external trigger. The trigger is like a sharp dagger digging into a soft spot of weakness in your psychological armor.

For example, a common emotional need is the need to be in control, which may have stemmed from not having control at an earlier stage of your life. These needs aren't bad; in fact, they have served you extremely well in the past. The reason you have them is because at some point in your life they allowed you to reach a certain goal or enabled a certain outcome. Your life experiences may have taught you that success depends on maintaining control, creating a safe environment, and surrounding yourself with people that appreciate your organization.

So what might happen if you feel that someone is subtly trying to wrestle control away from you, even if all they said was, "Well, what about *this* restaurant instead?" It might seem that your emotional need for control is being destroyed, and rather than deal with the discomfort of not having control, you make sure that you can keep it and that others know it. All of those options are unpleasant for everyone involved, especially when they occur loudly in a split second.

By the way, the list of emotional needs has a complete overlap with the list of negative associations from triggers: acceptance

- respect
- being understood
- being in control
- attention
- being needed or liked
- being treated fairly
- love
- being included
- predictability
- safety
- insecurity
- pride
- lack of confidence

Of course, the less these needs are fulfilled, the more your mind will actively search for situations or events that threaten them. Your mind becomes volatile, and you start to think only in terms of self-protection and security. Someone may try to simply assert their own opinion and you may react negatively because you see them as trying to cause havoc in your life.

At this point, you need to judge the truth of the situation. Are you really losing the need that you have? Is something actually being threatened, or is your reaction borne solely out of vicious defense? Only you can answer that, but in most cases, your reactions and emotional responses are far more about you (and your stepped-on emotional needs) than anyone else. We'll talk more about how to handle feelings of discomfort and emotional distress in the next chapter, but for now, all you need to do is ask yourself, "Why?"

You need to consciously acknowledge the need that is triggering your response or you will be enslaved to that need. If someone wants to try a new approach to an activity and asks you first, are you really giving up your control? Are you hanging on to a certain feeling rather than responding to the situation at hand? Can others indeed be trusted to take care of things and also not hurt you simultaneously? And for that matter, is the need for control as imperative to you as it once was? What will happen if you do not possess it at every moment of every day?

Understanding emotional triggers will have a very real impact on your life. You may not even realize that some of your negative habits are a result of triggers. If you find that you are following distinct patterns of emotional triggers and then a reactive negative event, then it is time to do something about it. Own your emotional needs and understand that you are acting out of pain and longing—everything that occurs afterward is just a projection of this. There's no reason that dealing with reminders of your past should be so painful and destructive.

The Emotional Spectrum

To better understand our emotional needs, we actually need one additional foundational skill: being *accurate* with our emotions.

In doing so, we must define the entire emotional spectrum so you know what you are dealing with, can guess where it came from, and then can react in the most optimal way. A doctor is only effective if she can diagnose the underlying sickness. Once that is achieved, she can prescribe medicine and actions to help that particular sickness. We can't seek to strengthen our emotional resolve if we are taking a stab in the dark at what emotional needs are feeling depleted.

Emotional granularity is what we are truly seeking when we think about accurately expressing and feeling our emotions. This is the process of understanding what you are feeling by putting a specific name on it. It seems insignificant, but you will be able to release some of the intensity of the emotion just by labeling it.

This is because there is a certain amount of tension from uncertainty and a lack of clarity about your feelings. Consider when you visit the doctor and have an illness, and the diagnosis is elusive. This is uncomfortable because you feel an intense lack of control and knowledge. Contrast that with immediately receiving a diagnosis and, subsequently, a plan for treatment.

People that have finely tuned feelings and are very in touch with their emotions are said to exhibit emotional granularity. It's not about being able to complicatedly label every emotion you have or just expand your vocabulary so that you can do this. It is about experiencing the world, and thus yourself, more precisely. By doing this, you will be able to better identify what it is exactly that you're feeling, and by identifying it, you will be able to understand the reasoning behind it.

Emotional granularity was coined in the 1990s by Lisa Feldman Barrett, who asked hundreds of volunteers to track and monitor their emotional experiences for weeks or months. All the participants in the study used the same vocabulary to define their emotions with standard words such as "sad," "angry," and "afraid." However, the study found that some people used the words to refer to distinct and differing experiences. Each word represented multiple emotional concepts and feelings. Others in the study lumped these words together under a single conceptual meaning, basically alluding to the feelings of being miserable.

According to Barrett, the greater the granularity, the "more precisely" you can experience yourself and your world. This means that you can pinpoint how you feel and better identify a solution. By using different words for different emotions and individualizing your vocabulary, there are many more benefits to your emotional health. We become what we label ourselves, and this can either help or hurt you.

People who were able to learn diverse emotional concepts were able to understand more finely tailored emotions. Emotional granularity can have a large influence on your health and well-being because it equips your brain to handle a wider range of emotions that you may experience. In other words, by knowing what you're feeling, you know better what the causes and underlying emotional needs are, and you know how to solve it.

For example, you may be feeling a combination of sadness, boredom, restlessness, and yearning, and without the proper understanding of your emotions, you may just generalize it as feeling sad.

But this does not solve the problem because it may not be exactly what you're feeling. However, this all changes if you have emotional granularity and are able to correctly identify your emotion as loneliness. Lumping emotions together means that you may not know how to deal with them, but identifying them all as distinct, independent emotions promotes understanding. Acting to fix a general feeling of sadness is a far different course of action than acting to fix loneliness.

The better your understanding of what it is exactly that you're experiencing, the more flexibility your brain has in anticipating or prescribing actions. It is easy to generalize or dismiss what you are feeling, but it is much more effective to give it some thought and pinpoint exactly what your emotional state is.

One step to take in increasing your emotional vocabulary is to take a look at the true spectrum of emotions. Quick, try to name as many emotions as you can. How many did you come up with? Here, the spectrum is represented by Robert Plutchik's wheel of emotions (courtesy of wired.com):

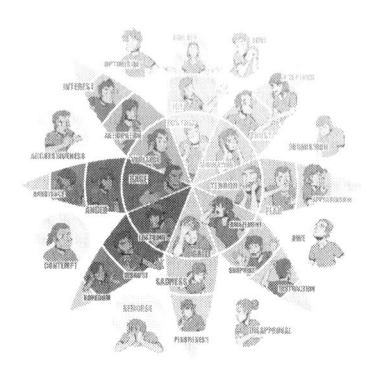

The purpose of this wheel is to provide a visual method for identifying a variety of emotions and to help relate them all to each other. Emotions on the outside, such as love, are a combination of two emotions in the petals beside them, in this case joy and trust. Similarly, awe is a combination of surprise and fear. In this way, you can view a range of different emotions and you can visually map which ones are similar and what emotions make up others. You may have been able to name only five emotions before seeing the wheel, but you can now see there are subtle differences and degrees for each. You can probably also imagine circumstances that would create each feeling and match the corresponding faces.

Understanding emotional diversity is fundamental to our well-being. A study led by Anthony Ong of Cornell University investigated the effect of emotion on health. The study suggested that happiness is too often considered the emotion most strongly connected to a healthier body. The researchers found that feeling a wide range of emotions—what they termed emotional diversity, or *emodiversity*—may be the link to better health. This includes negative emotions and is another powerful argument for understanding emotional granularity and familiarizing yourself with Plutchik's wheel.

Ong had participants keep a journal of their emotions for 30 days. The participants had to rate the extent to which they experienced 16 positive emotions that day. Happiness, enthusiasm, determination, pride, inspiration, and strength were among the positive emotions. They also recorded any negative emotions they experienced, such as sadness, anger, shame, and guilt. Emodiversity was measured by the number of different emotions felt by a person, the overall distribution, and the number of times each emotion was felt.

Ong found that people who experienced a wider range of emotions, including negative ones, were better at regulating emotions, keeping their cool, and refraining from using alcohol as a coping mechanism. He explained by comparing the emotions to a natural ecosystem, which is healthier when each various species serves its specific, functional role. If any one species becomes too dominant, it destroys the balance of the entire ecosystem and causes, for example, the dodo bird to go extinct.

Emodiversity similarly helps us prioritize and regulate our behavior so that we can cope and adapt to any given situation. By experiencing many different but specific emotions, there is more adaptive value than experiencing fewer emotions or more general ones. This is because the more specific emotions provide richer and more useful information to guide our decisions and how we face challenges.

For example, if you identify that you are feeling a variety of emotions such as anger, shame, and sadness, this will be more useful to you than just saying you feel "bad," which is a general term that doesn't provide you with much insight into how to solve the problem.

By specifying anger, you can then delve into what or who made you angry. By specifying shame, you are implying that you yourself have done something that you may regret. By specifying sadness, you may believe that the cause of your current emotional state shouldn't have happened and you want to fix the issue. All these points of action simply come from being able to identify your real emotions. If you had just stopped at feeling "bad," you may not have done anything at all. Indulging in the full range of negative emotions simply prepares you.

Admitting you have emotional triggers and needs is only the first step to emotional resilience and calm. This chapter takes the additional steps of understanding emotional granularity and the overall importance of attaching a name to feelings. Indulge in your emotions and feel the entire spectrum of possibilities. Your happiness depends on it.

Takeaways:

- When we talk about emotional resilience and calm, we are really talking about the emotional triggers that push us over the edge. The vast majority of the time, these triggers will be subtle and external and not at all proportionate (or even related) to the response they will create within you. This is the classic case of overreacting to a simple statement based on how it made you feel, not the actual substance.
- Of course, this is because our emotional needs are being exposed, poked, or prodded in an uncomfortable way. To escape this discomfort, we react by

lashing out, avoiding, or coping in a variety of other ways. Very few of these habits are healthy, and this sequence of events is what will lead to your unraveling and emotional instability.

- It's not enough to simply know your emotional needs; we need to gain emotional granularity into what is actually happening. A doctor can only treat a sickness if they know the actual cause, and Plutchik's wheel of emotions is a useful tool in labeling yourself and escaping the uncertainty of a general feeling of dread and discomfort. In fact, diversity of emotion helps us remain balanced and even-keeled.

Chapter 3. Recognize, Respond, and Regulate

Our emotions are not always reliable. Recall that they are geared toward ensuring the survival of our species, but that's a goal with somewhat lesser priority in daily life.

We know that suppressing them is not the answer and that you should allow yourself to feel even your darkest of feelings so that you can release them. But there is a time and a place for indulging in all of the emotional needs we have discussed, and sometimes you may just not be in the right situation to do so. Regulating your emotions means dealing with your emotional needs in a healthy and socially acceptable way. This chapter will explain how you can release your emotions in ways that won't make you embark on a downward spiral.

Emotions are a constant part of our lives. Every minute of every day we will feel something, and our emotions can change in an instant. There are highs and lows that you experience every day, and how you deal with them can significantly affect your mental state and well-being. Our ability to regulate the vast number of emotions that you feel also affects how the people in your life perceive you. It can be difficult when you are caught up in these moments to regulate your emotions and think of the consequences, but the more you do it, the more it becomes habitual.

The first and foremost way of thinking about emotional resilience and calm is the *react versus response* model. It is succinctly summed up in the image below:

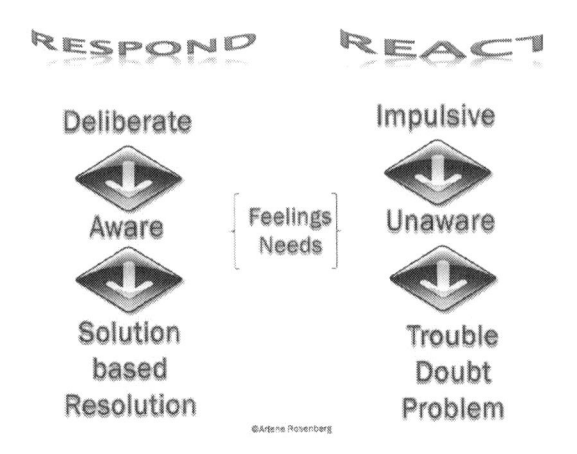

```
RESPOND              REACT

Deliberate           Impulsive
    ⬇                   ⬇
 Aware  [Feelings]   Unaware
        [ Needs  ]
    ⬇                   ⬇
 Solution            Trouble
  based               Doubt
 Resolution          Problem
          ©Arlene Rosenberg
```

Overall, emotional regulation begins and ends with this image. To *react* to a situation means a complete lack of regulation because there is no thought. It is impulsive, short-term thinking. If we touch a hot stove, we react by yanking our hand away as quickly as possible to avoid a burn. All we are focused on is immediate relief, and rational thought is not possible during this phase.

To *respond* is to take time to consider the alternatives and make a decision based on the information you have. It may not always be the right one, but you won't be acting on impulse or elevated emotions. This is where rational thought lives, and either healthy coping mechanisms can be utilized or the emotions are given time to process and freeze over. It isn't just about controlling what you feel, but also about thinking rationally about what the best course of action is. Focus less on your intense emotional impulses and more on desired outcomes and rational decisions.

This is obviously impossible in the case of the hot stove, but it's very, very rare that we are encountering the emotional equivalent of a hot stove. The problem is that we continually view any transgression as something that requires an immediate reaction, and this becomes hardcoded into our habits until we are a walking volcanic reaction (and not response). Thus, the important part to recognize here is that you are probably so used to reacting that this chain of events cannot be mentally separated for you.

For instance, when you wake up in the morning, you use the bathroom, brush your teeth, wash your face, and put your clothes on. Is it likely that you'll forget any of these elements? No—because just like your emotional reactions, they cannot be mentally separated from the trigger. They are linked in a way that is so natural now that you cannot imagine any other way.

Let's imagine an example of a fight between a couple about where to spend the holidays. In this situation, it may have been that you both wanted to spend the holidays with your own family and that they wanted you to spend it with theirs. A reaction to this might mean that you immediately discount the other person's opinions and assume that they want to control your actions or that your family doesn't matter. Without even thinking about the purpose and weight behind your partner's words, you simply begin to throw blame, feel anger, and then pick a fight about priorities. (Of course, there are some emotional needs that are being exposed here.)

Responding would be entirely different. The first step of responding is to take a moment to think and ask *why*. The answer may be that they haven't seen their family in a far longer time. What if they have a family member that is in ill health? What if they dislike your family as your mother always lobs passive-aggressive statements about their weight? This brief pause of consideration allows you to understand the other person's perspective and allows a rational discussion where both people will be satisfied or, at the very least, a conclusion will be reached. Responding is almost never *easy*, but it is *simple*.

Differentiating between reacting and responding is the first step toward true emotional regulation and keeping even-keeled. It's the first place where self-awareness can be your best friend.

A Regulation Framework

After one or two instances where you've chosen the path of responding versus reacting, you may begin to see the value of keeping your emotions in check. It's one of the most difficult tasks in the world, especially if you don't have much practice with it. This is the first and arguably toughest step, and there isn't much I can tell you about it other than to breathe deeply, make sure not to act when your heart rate is elevated, insert as much time as possible between the external trigger and your response, and continue to ask yourself on a constant basis, "Why am I feeling this?"

Soon, you'll require a new set of tools for greater emotional control. You'll find that you are responding versus reacting, and yet your emotional state may not be upbeat or happy. You are still annoyed and peeved, even though you haven't acted out. This is where a framework for emotional *regulation* comes in handy.

Of course, some emotional responses require no regulation—mostly positive ones. Laughing at a friend's joke or crying in a sad film are all acceptable behaviors in their specific contexts. If an emotion is appropriate and helps you feel better, then there is no need to regulate.

For example, your impatience and anger at waiting in a long line. It might make you feel better, but it is neither appropriate nor productive. How can you regulate something like this by either expressing this frustration in alternative means or regaining your emotional composure? Stanford psychologist J.J. Gross came up with a five-step method for regulating emotion.

The first step is to select the situation.

This means that you should seek to avoid situations that trigger unwanted emotions in the first place whenever possible. If you have an allergy to peanuts, you can simply stay away from them.

Imagine that you have recently decided to partake in a marathon. You've been training hard, eating healthily, and increasing your endurance. However, maybe you find that you lose motivation when you see others at the gym and they seem to be running so much faster than you or lifting so much more than you. This is where you can employ this step. Maybe you will go for more runs outside instead of in the gym.

It doesn't mean that you are escaping your problems. It simply means that to keep your emotions up, you chose not to surround yourself with things that might bring you negativity. Remove yourself from dangerous situations so you don't have to regulate at all. You have more of a say than you think.

The next step is to modify the situation.

This is when you cannot employ step one. Let's say that you work late and choose not to run outside because it's cold and dark. You know that at the gym you normally have feelings of inadequacy and you wish to reduce this. This is where you have to face the situation you have been trying to avoid, so you need to modify it to reduce its impact on you. You modify the situation to insulate your emotions by actively changing the terms for success. You alter your expectations to something that is more realistic and doesn't set you up for failure. Just because you can't go as fast as someone doesn't mean you can't run for as long. If you adjust the rules and make it so you are competing only with yourself, then you are in a can't-lose situation. After all, you are the one writing the rules for yourself—why do you need to be so strict and harsh?

The third step is to shift your focus.

When you can't avoid or modify a situation, you can always change what you focus your attention on. If you're upset by something, you fixate on it to your own detriment. Instead of being preoccupied by runners that are faster than you, shift your focus to the gym-goers who are much, much faster than you. You can also shift your focus to yourself and your own running—perhaps you aren't running so fast because you're always distracted and discouraged. Concentrate on improving yourself and reaching your own goals instead of beating someone else.

You don't need to compete with anyone but yourself. Whatever negative thoughts seem to be taking your attention, switch to positive ones. See the brighter side and try to feel gratitude for what you still have and others don't. It's quite difficult to feel both gratitude and emotional turmoil simultaneously.

Step four is to change your thoughts.

At the core of our deepest emotions are the beliefs that drive them. By knowing this, you can change your emotions by changing the beliefs that sustain them. Your negative belief is that everyone at the gym is judging you for your failures—therefore, your emotions will reflect that.

This is where you need to change your thoughts. To do this, think about how you view others at the gym. Most of the time, you don't really care what they do, or you think their performance is better than yours. By that reasoning, what if they feel the same about you? Believe that people don't judge and aren't even paying attention to you, and your emotions will follow and relax.

What is the evidence that your beliefs are true, and what is the evidence that they are not? If it helps, literally make a list and tally up the score.

The fifth and final step of emotion regulation, when all else fails, is to change your response.

This is true regulation. This is when no other steps of this process work and you find yourself feeling without limits. Maybe you feel utterly destroyed, decide to give up, and are very close to tears or rage. Take a deep breath to gather yourself, close your eyes, and pause. Gather your inner reserve and force yourself at least to change your facial expression and *keep it in*. You're still in react mode.

Obviously, you won't be able to. I did mention that emotional suppression was unhealthy, but this is different because you are trying to make it to the point where you can respond instead of react. When we can reflect a bit more, often we will find perspective and a different and healthier way to respond. By pausing in your tracks and taking a few moments to let them dwell on your emotions, you will find that you can actively regulate them.

Another similar model is called the STOPP Method, created by Carol Vivyan. STOPP stands for:

- stop
    - simply pause and try not to let yourself be overcome by emotion
- take a breath
    - breathe deeply to keep your heart rate in check and notice your breathing in a conscious effort to keep it slow and measured
- observe
    - ask what is going through your mind, determine where your focus lies, discover what you are reacting to, and try to name the

feelings that are swirling through your brain
- pull back for perspective
    - ask yourself what is really happening, try to incorporate different perspectives, understand how little it ultimately matters in your life, and remember to not instantly see disaster
- practice what works
    - proceed with the best action you can take for the time being, remember your values, make sure you are responding rather than reacting, and focus on your main goals for the situation at hand

Remember that inserting a delay between our intense emotions and our responses is always the end goal.

None of the steps in these emotional regulation frameworks are easy. And at some point, the thrust of the next section, simply increasing your tolerance to emotional discomfort and anxiety becomes a necessary step toward resilience and calm. The more you can take, the less you need to regulate. You'll recognize some common elements from the regulation framework we've just discussed.

Distress Tolerance

Distress is a natural part of life. Every person at some point or another needs to face discomfort and anxiety; it's not a question of whether you'll have to endure it, but *when*. Fortunately, emotional resilience is something that can be learned and cultivated with a plan and frequent practice.

While many might choose to focus on avoiding emotional discomfort or arranging a life where they don't have to experience it, a truly resilient person trusts in their own ability to withstand distress and not just survive, but thrive. Most importantly, having a higher degree of distress tolerance makes you hardier; you won't even have to use coping or self-awareness tools as often, because you simply won't reach those heightened negative emotions as frequently. Greater tolerance to distress and anxiety can be mastered over time using just a few simple steps.

Step 1: Identify your triggers

It always goes back to the triggers, doesn't it? Whether this is a particular situation, an event, a person, words, memories, thoughts, body sensations, sounds, or images, a trigger is like a bell that starts us off down the path of distress. Sometimes, a pattern of distress can happen swiftly and without our conscious awareness, leaving us clueless as to why we're suddenly upset. One moment you're feeling fine and going about your day, and the next you feel the escalating sense of panic, anger, or sadness. But what happened?

If you look closely, you can always identify the precise stimulus that caused your emotional response. It's tempting to think that emotional control and mastery is all about wrestling emotions once they're already in full swing. But with practice, you can start to see the small seeds of distress *before* they sprout into overwhelming emotion that's hard to get a grip on.

Imagine a woman heads home for the Christmas holidays to be with her family. She starts the visit feeling calm and balanced and has told herself that she'll keep her cool even though her family is notorious for heated arguments and upsets during the holidays. Despite feeling okay for a while, she soon notices her mother's messy kitchen and feels herself getting agitated at how chaotic the food preparation is, with everyone talking over each other and weighing in on how best to prepare the Christmas meal. Then she notices she's starting to feel a bit physically warm, given that the fire is crackling away in the next room and several people in warm jumpers are bustling in and out of the kitchen. Finally, her father makes a hurtful comment about the way she is chopping onions, and like a dam breaking, she suddenly feels extremely angry and upset and snaps at everyone. In other words, she's distressed.

Rewind the situation and it's clear that there are several triggers instigating these feelings of anger and unhappiness. These are both external (noise and bustle, untidiness, criticism from loved ones) and internal (the feeling of chaos and stress, feeling too warm, not feeling good enough, or perhaps recalling negative memories and associations from childhood).

Triggers can be literally anything. Anniversaries, money problems, arguing with your family or spouse, workplace conflict, going to the doctor, taking an exam, falling ill, having to compete with others, thinking about the future, being rejected... The list goes on and on.

How do you find out what your *own* triggers are? A good way to think about this is to look at past behavior and try to understand what's reliably caused distressed for you before. This takes a degree of awareness in the moment, but can you notice any patterns in what occurs immediately before you become emotionally overwhelmed?

The great thing about becoming aware of your triggers is that when they occur, they give you an opportunity to stop and take notice of what is happening. This gives you the option to step in and take action before becoming overwhelmed with strong emotions.

Step 2: Pay attention to your warning signs

Of course, a trigger is just a trigger—it's our response to it that makes all the difference. A warning sign can be thought of as any indication that you are having trouble dealing with some emotional distress. Again, these can be thoughts, emotions, or the urge to behave in a particular way. They indicate that distress is underway and that you are dealing with strong unpleasant emotions.

What could happen at this point is that you resort to "escape methods" to try to avoid the distress. These kinds of behaviors can be as varied as the triggers that they're designed to avoid. They can include seeking assurance, distracting yourself, resorting to substances or overeating, oversleeping, or simply avoiding the stressful situation completely.

In the example of the woman above, the mounting emotional stress she experienced leads to a very clear warning sign: snapping at the people in the kitchen with her. Whereas the triggers might have been small bells, warning signs are more like blaring fire alarms. Warning signs are not just actions, however. They can be thoughts (for example, "I can't do this" or "I'm a failure") or feelings (for example, irritation, panic, depression, shame, or jealousy) or even physical body sensations (for example, fatigue, shaking, a knot in the stomach, tension, or tearfulness).

It can be difficult to clearly see distress as it unfolds in the moment, precisely because distress is so unpleasant and we're often seeking ways to avoid it at all costs. That's why the regular practice of distress tolerance will sharpen your ability to zoom in on your unique triggers and exactly how they affect you.

Step 3: Forego your escape mechanism and do the opposite

Step 3 is where your distress tolerance plan really comes to life. Being triggered and experiencing overwhelming emotional, mental, and physical sensations can force us down the path of automatic habits designed to make us feel better. However, *escape behaviors* seldom give us the opportunity to develop resilience and grow as people, and frequently the escape behaviors themselves are harmful to us.

For the woman in our example, snapping at family members is only likely to put them on edge and in turn feed the chaos and stress in the kitchen, unintentionally making matters worse. Other escape behaviors can be even more damaging—for example, binge-eating, alcohol abuse, or avoiding doing tasks at work that will only become worse with procrastination.

Though escape behaviors feel irresistible in the moment, and they may sincerely feel like our only solution at times, they are not ultimately adaptive and come from a place of avoidance, weakness, denial, and escape rather than confidence and strength to deal with what life throws our way.

How do you know what your escape behaviors are? This part of the process might be the easiest to identify since they'll be those actions you feel strongly compelled to do when in the thick of an overwhelming emotional reaction. Many people get intense cravings for sweet things after an upsetting argument or feel compelled to get up and leave the room if the situation feels utterly hopeless and overpowering. Look closely at those behaviors you feel unable to resist when emotionally overwhelmed and you'll likely learn something about your escape patterns.

The trick is then to deliberately and consciously commit to doing the opposite of that behavior, which invariably means to seek calm, not escape, and remain in the situation and emotion.

Triggers and warning signs are invitations to become aware in the moment and make the (admittedly difficult!) choice to take a different path. Luckily, this gets easier and easier the more you practice it. You might, for example, choose to quietly tell yourself, "I will stay with my feelings right now instead of trying to avoid them." You can silently say this sentence to yourself again and again in your mind, say it out loud, write it out in a journal, or even share your sentiment with someone close. The point is to bring your actions out into the open and convert old automatic habit into conscious action that you have a choice in.

Knowing what your triggers and warning signs are ahead of time can help immensely with this. If you know that you are prone to thinking thoughts like "this is unbearable" and resorting to self-harm to distract yourself, you may choose to instead recite a little mantra to yourself: "I *can* bear this. I am choosing to stay with my feelings and not escape them."

Step 4: Accept your distress and discomfort

Once you have identified your triggers and warning signs, and once you have made the commitment to stay present with whatever emotional responses emerge in you, the only thing left to do is follow through with it. Of course, this can seem easier said than done!

This part of the process can feel counterintuitive and, by its very nature, can be emotionally overwhelming. But again, frequent practice along with a willingness to stay with what emerges will eventually help you develop a tolerance for unpleasant emotions.

Firstly, in order to accept an emotion, you need to be able to correctly recognize that it is occurring. Take some time to be still with that sensation, whatever it is. Try not to rush in to deny or avoid it, and remember that there's no need to embrace it either or pretend it isn't there. Simply give yourself and the emotion space to expand, and watch. What can you feel in your body? What sort of thoughts are in your mind? How do those thoughts make you feel? Why is this happening to you?

This exercise can be done during a more formal meditation, or you can simply choose to pause and take a moment out of your daily life to gather yourself and become aware of your emotions.

Next, try to gain some distance from the emotion by using imagery. It's so easy to get "swallowed up" by an emotion, feeling as though it is us and that we are completely identified with it. But emotions are temporary and passing. Can you find a way to let the emotion be what it is without getting carried away with it?

For example, our example woman may imagine that all the chatter and chaos and negative emotion of the family holidays is like a dark cloud of tangled words that she can wrap up in a beautiful pink balloon, where, once inside, it goes silent and peaceful. She can then stand outside of these emotions and hold them on a string, apart from herself. Another person might imagine that their sadness and overwhelming depression is really a small, tired person who just wants to sit at the table for a little while. By sitting across from this person and allowing it to speak without getting upset about its existence, we can start to gain some distance and detachment. This is the beginning of emotional mastery.

As you engage with your emotions, whatever they are and in whatever image you have given them, pay close attention to your breath. Being focused on the simple inhale and exhale of your breath can ground you in the moment and remind you to stay anchored in the present. Wait out your emotional spike and see what is on the other side.

Part of the practice of learning to tolerate emotional distress is understanding that it is a practice (i.e., not something you master all at once and never have to look at again). If you are aware and accepting of the fact that you *will* experience emotional comebacks, you can remain calm when they occur and appreciate them for what they are: an opportunity to try again to turn away from avoidance and escape behavior and reaffirm your commitment to yourself.

Emotional strength and the ability to calmly withstand even the most unpleasant emotions is like a muscle: the more you exercise it, the stronger it gets. So be grateful for every opportunity you have to exercise it. If you feel strong emotions arising again, watch yourself closely. Are you frustrated with yourself for not "doing it right"? Are you impatient with the process, feeling like you should have succeeded with it sooner? Great! Take these feelings themselves and feed them back into your practice. Remind yourself of your commitment to doing the opposite of your escape behaviors. Remind yourself that you can and will stay with feelings and that all feelings, no matter how unpleasant, will pass. Sit with them and observe that, past an initial period of high stress and anxiety, they aren't overwhelming experiences— merely uncomfortable.

Step 5: Making friends with distress

We are all individuals, and nobody is going to experience distress in quite the same way. The only way to truly understand your own emotional patterns and behaviors is to get in there directly and become aware of them.

These five steps can be thought of as a closed sequence that improves and refines itself every time you go through a cycle. Every time you are able to successfully soothe yourself without avoidance/escape behaviors, take note and remember how you did it. Next time you are in a similar position, you can pull these activities, thoughts, or ideas out of your emotional inventory and use them. In essence, you are building greater awareness of yourself and slowly removing the behavior from the realm of passive, reactionary, and unconscious into the realm of deliberate, conscious action that really serves you.

This final step is about taking stock of what works. This can be actively making a list of behaviors that you want to practice or simply taking a moment to quietly acknowledge progress when it happens. Make a note of words of encouragement, mantras, or images that help you get into the state of mind you're trying to achieve. Write them down somewhere you can easily access, or maybe try carrying a small object that encourages you to stay mindful.

In fact, once you begin to feel more in control, you can start to actively seek out exposure to distress in order to gain practice and strengthen your resilience. Though this may seem scary, in a way, it gives you more control to engineer situations that from the outset have you feeling prepared and confident.

If you'd like to do this, start with your triggers, and think of a situation that may make you feel distressed. Of course, it may backfire to throw you in the deep end of distress—instead, think of an ultimate goal that you'd like to achieve and then set up a few gradual steps and smaller goals you can achieve to reach that. This "exposure ladder" is a series of manageable steps that increase in increments. Each step might involve spending more and more time in the distressing situation, or it may entail increasing the intensity of a sensation or an interaction with a triggering person.

As an example, a man might have trouble with watching certain highly charged news shows or movies as a trigger and resort to overeating as an escape behavior. He commits to telling himself that he can, in fact, tolerate the feelings of depression and hopelessness this brings up. He sets himself a goal: to be able to watch a full news program without overeating to soothe himself. He starts with smaller steps. First, he watches five minutes. Then he watches two five-minute segments with a break. Then he watches ten uninterrupted minutes. And so on.

Whether you choose to practice an emotional exposure ladder or simply want to do your action plan when distress naturally rears its head, if you can stay with the emotion in the present, breathe, reorient your behavior, and reward any successes, you essentially train yourself toward greater emotional control and stability.

Takeaways:

- Now that we've got an understanding of emotional triggers, needs, pain, and how they all interact with each other, we must talk about how to deal with them. How can we inject self-awareness into our lives, recognize what's happening, and keep the volcano (us) from erupting? The first model to think about is responding versus reacting. When we touch a hot stove, we are reacting without thought, instinctually, and to protect ourselves. This is rarely necessary from an emotional standpoint, and yet we find ourselves similarly

volatile to a volcano instead of pausing a beat to think and then respond.
- Next, we should think about a framework for regulation that plays with the emotional triggers and needs we have discussed. This consists of selecting the situation (avoiding triggers), modifying the situation (decreasing triggers), shifting focus (ignoring triggers), changing thoughts (changing the trigger), and changing response (reacting less to a trigger).
- This leads directly to the next point of distress tolerance. Sometimes we are indeed too prone to flying off the handle; we are overly sensitive in a way that makes us unpredictable and fragile. Thus, we need to work on increasing our tolerance to distress and anxiety. This has common elements with the framework for regulation, but it focuses more on foregoing the comforting escape mechanisms you use and staying in the situation and emotion. The purpose is to accept anxiety and distress, withstand the major emotional spike surrounding it, and stay with it

until it subsides and you realize that you are still doing fine.

Chapter 4. Cutting the Cycle

So far, we've talked about the purpose of emotions, common triggers and the emotional needs that underlie them, and some ways to respond and regulate in healthier ways.

These all constitute important knowledge about your inner workings, but at some level, they are just Band-Aids that we can apply over the emotional pain or discomfort you feel. The true cure to emotional haphazardness is self-awareness and understanding the origins of your emotions. It isn't just about why you feel a certain way, but also about how that feeling took root. Only when you understand the entire sequence of events, from outside (trigger) to inside (emotional need) to outside (coping mechanism), can you hope to cut the cycle short.

Sometimes we find ourselves falling into a loop where we are simply in an autopilot state of acting and thinking, which will always lead to undesirable outcomes. Your feelings get hurt, you shout and react, and you compound your negative feelings with guilt and shame. You might think you are engaging in the framework of emotional regulation, and you might think that you are responding rather than reacting. But how can you know?

These automated actions are very difficult to see in the heat of the moment because we are so used to doing them without thinking. This is why building self-awareness and understanding the patterns of your thought and behavior are essential for emotional resilience. Without this, you will only be able to address the symptoms and not the cause.

There are a few tools for this, and they emulate talk therapy in some ways because they force you to really analyze your actions and answer questions that you'd rather not. You'll recognize a few elements of these tools from prior chapters, but there is always a different perspective in each new tool that can assist with self-awareness.

The ABC Loop

The ABC Loop is a classic behavioral therapy technique that considers all the elements that contribute to a behavior. It stands for antecedent (A), behavior (B), and consequence (C). The middle section, the behavior, is often called the behavior of interest, and the technique works by looking at the before and after to understand why the behavior in the middle occurred. It's also what you want to examine and regulate or control—hence, the increased scrutiny on it. In isolating these three elements, we can begin to understand what is actually happening in the external world and how it relates to the emotions we feel.

Let's begin with the antecedent. This is the environment, the events, or circumstances preceding the behavior of interest. Anything that happens before the event that may contribute to the behavior would fall into this category. When identifying the antecedents, consider where and when they are occurring, during what activity, with whom they occurred, and what any others were doing at the time. Write down a mental snapshot of everything you can recall; you never know what might be pertinent to the ABC Loop.

For example, perhaps you are someone who finds yourself constantly arguing with your parents. You might realize that most of the time you don't even agree with what you're arguing with, but you do it anyway. You want to stop this behavior so you think about the last time it occurred. Set the scene first. In this situation—dinner at your parents' house, early afternoon—things were going fine, the television was playing, the topic of the future came up, and you were talking about your job and your career goals. This is the antecedent.

Then we move onto the behavior, which is the focus of this technique. This behavior can either be pivotal, which leads to further undesirable behaviors, or distracting, which can interfere with your own life or the lives of others. In this case, the behavior is uncontrollable anger, which is pivotal because it causes stress and irrationality in other parts of your life, too. It is important to describe the behavior in full when looking back in hindsight. There is some overreaction on your part, a complete lack of listening and validation on their part, and the feeling that you must make yourself heard. In this situation, there are raised voices, dramatic gestures, insults thrown, and intentionally vicious comments being said, most of which were irrelevant to the actual argument.

Last is the consequence of the behavior. This outcome is important because it is often one that reinforces the behavior. If the consequence is one that is genuinely undesirable, most unwanted behaviors will not be repeated, but if there is some sort of reward that is incidentally received, then the behavior will continue.

In this case, the outcome may be that one of your parents, usually your mother, leaves the room upset and the dinner is cut short, whereby you then go home. However, you might feel that you have "won" the encounter by making your mother back down, and this would be a positive reinforcement to continue engaging in this sort of behavior. But is it actually positive if everyone has been worked up to a frenzy and is feeling the adrenal residue of a loud argument? You got a little piece of satisfaction, but it's probably not a net positive interaction here.

Now comes the analysis of the ABC. The antecedent, as mentioned before, is the family dinner. It is important to mention the last thing to happen before the behavior. In this case, it was questions about career goals and aspirations. Already we have identified an important factor of the situation. Considering this is the last casual question before the argument, it is clear that this is the catalyst. If you are looking back at your own event and are able to identify the catalyst, consider why it affects you so much. Do you always react in the same way?

If you can identify what it is that catalyzes a behavior you want to stop, then you can focus on it and actively try to redirect your behavior when you encounter a similar situation again. This is where we also start to think about emotional triggers and needs. Why is this so triggering for you, and what need is it uncovering that isn't fulfilled? This doesn't happen with everyone, just your parents; why are they triggering you, and what emotional need is intensified with them specifically?

The next thing to observe is the behavior itself. In this case, it is uncontrollable yelling, but it can be a whole range of different ones. Think about why it is that you choose this behavior. In this case, maybe you feel as if you're not being heard.

Maybe you want to exercise some control or authority or overcompensate because you are feeling cornered. Whatever the reasoning behind it, think about what purpose it serves. Usually, this is a coping or defense mechanism. But is it actually helping? Your purpose here is actually to make sure that your emotional need is either defended or fulfilled—is your behavior working toward that goal?

If not, is there another way to behave to get a better outcome with regard to your emotions? Even if it is something as simple as taking a moment to calm down, leaving the situation, or telling someone that you are not in an emotional state to continue, find a way to redirect your behavior so that you produce a different emotional outcome.

The last thing to consider is the consequence. If it is a recurring behavior, then that must mean you get some reward out of it. In this scenario, your mother has left the scene directly after the argument and you are forced to go home. Maybe this is exactly what you want—to spend less time with your parents. Maybe you just want them to support your career, and when it seems they aren't, then you don't wish to be there anymore. Maybe you want to score a "win" over them or be the last person standing and have the last word.

Have you learned anything from this experience, or is the consequence simply that you will double down on your behaviors from before? Do you feel compelled to change anything to make it so that your antecedent isn't triggered even worse next time and the behavior doesn't keep growing in proportion? An easy question to ask is the following: does the consequence make you feel good or bad?

So now consider the overall outcome of this event that we have analyzed with the ABC Loop. We can see that we are emotionally triggered by some combination of our parents and the topic of the future and that there is a particular emotional need or pain that comes out in this setting (antecedent). Next, we see that our behaviors are a somewhat unhealthy response to this emotional need and pain and aren't necessarily about the topic or setting by themselves (behavior). Finally, we observe that we've defended our emotional need and pain so hard that we cause turmoil in the relationship (consequence), and though this is a small victory for your emotional shields, it only makes the antecedent and behavior more likely to be amplified in the future.

How can you change this sequence of events to make sure it doesn't happen again in the future? It always starts with questioning yourself and asking why you feel such emotional pain—this is what leads to the behavior and then to the consequence, where the cycle repeats all over again. You can either cut off the conversation before the emotional pain reaches a boiling point or you can make sure that the behavior is something that soothes you and helps you cope.

For instance, if all you want is to be supported in your decisions, have a conversation that deals with this and leave it when it doesn't. If there is something you don't want to discuss, tell your parents that there are things you would prefer to be off-limits and you might discuss when you're ready; leave it if they keep pushing you.

The ABC Loop helps you understand how to cut the cycle of lack of emotional control, and it explains why things tend to get worse over time, not better. It gives you the exact blueprint for better emotional resilience and calm: avoid or alter situations that can turn into an antecedent, and attempt to choose healthier behaviors when you are triggered.

Emotional Dashboarding

Emotional dashboarding is a similar process to the ABC Loop. It also encourages stepping back from a situation to review your actions and reactions to break into your autopilot. While the introspective approach of emotional dashboarding is the same as the ABC Loop, there are a couple of more incremental steps:

SITUATION/ FACTS	THOUGHTS	EMOTIONS	BODILY SENSATIONS	IMPULSES/ ACTIONS
Example: Project due tomorrow	*"I don't feel like doing this." "I shouldn't have to."*	*Sadness, boredom, irritation*	*Heaviness, fatigue*	*Go to sleep, eat, space out*

Situation. Jot down the literal facts of the situation—details that couldn't be argued by any observer. This means leaving out opinions and existing prejudice or bias. This will help you understand the circumstances around your bad moods or emotional outbursts.

- A project is due tomorrow.
- Your spouse's family is arriving for the holidays.
- You're assigned a new supervisor.
- You've moved to a new place after a breakup and are invited to a party.

Thoughts. Recall the personal interpretations and thoughts that went through your mind when the first feelings of distress or avoidance came up. These are the beliefs and thoughts that are triggered by external events. Often, these are far more volatile and violent than the following examples because they lead directly to the

next step of emotions and emotional needs and pain. Really try to articulate your inner monologue, as it can literally tell you everything you need to know about your mental and emotional state.
- "I don't feel like doing this"; "I shouldn't have to."
- "Last year they seemed judgmental about the appearance of our house."
- "I've heard bad things about this person from people who've worked under him."
- "I'm not sure I'm ready to mingle with strangers in an unfamiliar place."

Emotions. Take a measure of the feelings you experienced during this conflict using only single emotion words. For our purposes, be sure to also think about the emotional need or pain that is being invoked. Make the connection from the external actions to your thoughts and to your emotions. See them as a continual cycle, a cycle that we are trying to understand and ultimately cut in favor of something healthier or happier.
- sadness, boredom, irritation
- resentment, disfavor, annoyance

- anxiety, fear, concern
- dejection, tension, uneasiness

When naming your reactions, ask yourself three times why these emotions came up. The repetition of the question will encourage you to go as deep as possible and get to the root of the problem. In the first example, what mental picture caused the sadness about the late project—fear that it won't be good enough? Is the boredom because you feel it's a routine that keeps recurring? Are you irritated because there was a social event you would rather have done tonight?

Bodily sensations. Mark down the physical sensations you felt when experiencing the conflict. These can add clarity to your emotions, because while we can lie to ourselves, our bodies can only react and will almost always tell the truth.
- heaviness, fatigue
- stomach upset, headache
- shoulder tension, increased heartbeat
- lightness in head, slight tremors in hands

Be as literal as possible in describing bodily sensations. Avoid metaphors like "My heart was jumping out of my chest"—instead, say, "I felt my heartbeat accelerating." Sometimes our bodies know something far sooner than our brains can register.

Impulses/actions. Write down your first instincts of what you wanted to do to relieve or avoid the conflict—things that made you feel good, distracted you, or minimized your attention to the preceding sensations. If these are relatively benign or healthy, that's a good thing. However, if your first impulses are to react with rage or lash out at someone, then you know a chord has been struck. Something is happening within you, and it is being demonstrated through your actions.

- go to sleep, eat, space out
- watch TV, surf online
- do "busy" work, make phone calls, scream a little bit
- drink alcohol, walk outside

Like the ABC Loop, the practice of emotional dashboarding produces a sequence of events that can be broken down and assessed like a fictional story. Why did this happen, how can we prevent it, and what elements seem to be your downfall? The dashboard adds a few internal elements—internal conflicts and physical sensations—that play the same role that "motivation" serves in fiction. Recognizing those alterations in your feelings and thoughts can help you identify them when they come up again.

One method may seem more appropriate than the other, depending on your circumstances. You may want to use the ABC Loop when initially coming across a conflict, then the dashboard if it happens again or gets worse. If you sense your spouse's family being passive-aggressive or judgmental at your house for the first time, you may choose to run an ABC Loop first. If it happens again in another situation, you might want to run through the dashboard to see if you can gather additional insight about your moods and reactions.

It may simply be easier or more efficient just to execute an ABC Loop. Or perhaps your discomfort is so acute that you'd rather run the emotional dashboard. With honest self-inquiry, either method can help you make headway in discovering patterns and identifying troubling behaviors to change.

Healthy Self-Talk

The habit of healthy self-talk is the final way we discuss cutting the cycle of being controlled by our emotions.

In reality, self-talk is responsible for creating just about all of our emotions. This is because self-talk literally creates the perspectives and interpretations we have about the external world, and those filter directly into the emotions we feel. It doesn't have to be out loud; it can just be a silent communication in your mind. Self-talk is great when it is positive and reinforces constructive thoughts, but that's not what brings us here. We're here because our self-talk is self-defeating, negative, and makes us spiral out of control when we don't have to. It is our internal dialogue, and most of all, it is our choice and completely within our control.

So we never *have* to spiral out of control. But imagine someone who is applying for a job and doesn't believe they will get it. They think they are unqualified and can't seem to see their own value or skills. During the interview, they deflect praise and chalk it up to luck or the work of others. They keep thinking that this job is out of their reach, and in the end, they have acted in a way to make that true. They don't get the job. This disappointment makes them feel even worse about their abilities and self-esteem, and the spiral begins.

But there are many conscious choices in where this person ends up. Contrast that to someone who fully believes they are qualified—over-qualified, even. They can talk about their accomplishments without shying away, and they will list each of their applicable skills and experiences. They tell themselves the company would be lucky to hire them, and in the end, they get the job.

That is the difference between healthy and unhealthy self-talk. The first person generally feels poorly about themselves, which means all of their emotional needs and pains are being focused on. When you tell yourself something time after time, eventually you start to believe it, and it becomes true. They are creating a reality where they are emotionally unstable and fragile. In turn, we can actually tell ourselves something positive and uplifting, and eventually start to believe that as well.

It may not seem like it's a choice, but that's because it's so deeply rooted in our identities. It's a *narrative* that we've told ourselves since we were young, and it's almost impossible to separate from objective reality.

We all have our own personal narratives that shape who we are. Everyone in the world is the sum total of their own personal narratives. You would not be the person you are today if you didn't have the same childhood, the same struggles, the same failures, and the same successes. When someone asks you to tell them your life story, what is it that you tell them? What do you focus on and what do you leave out? You are the one who assigns all the meaning there is to your life and experience. No one else can determine what you think or feel. This is your narrative, and it is essential to make it empowering and positive while still being accurate and descriptive.

To regulate your emotions better, you need to recognize your personal narrative and change it. You are the sole person that defines your narrative, so you are the sole person who dictates how it should proceed. Changing your narrative isn't about changing your life; it's about the way you perceive it.

There are two types of narratives for our purposes: a disempowering one and an empowering one. Most of us tend to skew toward the disempowering narrative, but the empowering narrative is what gives us emotional regulation and resilience—especially if part of our narrative is the fact that we are indeed emotionally resilient. There are four steps to this.

The first is to identify your current story. How would you describe the narrative that you're telling yourself? Think about the words you are using and the emotional impact behind them. Are they only descriptive, and if so, what are they describing? Think about the feelings generated from your story and what parts you are drawn to and what parts have more meaning. ***My narrative is that I'm a survivor, and I will take control of everything around me because that's how I can ensure that I will survive. I can't really depend on anyone.***

The second is to evaluate the content of your story. Are you being empowered or disempowered? Is it a story of limiting belief? Does your story boost you up, empower you to succeed, and strive to build you up and push you forward, or does your story focus on the struggles, the failures, the disempowering moments, and the constant hardships? What are you downplaying and emphasizing from a bystander's perspective? Are you ignoring your talents and fixating on the rare times you falter? The focus of the story is what defines its effect. ***The survivor narrative is both empowering and disempowering. It makes me feel like I can do anything myself, but it is disempowering because it makes me so rigid and frankly scared of losing control. Control is everything, and I can spiral if I perceive I don't have it.***

Third is to characterize the outcomes of your story. This requires complete honesty. What does your story do to you? You must be able to honestly say if it is helping you or only hindering your progress. Does it serve as fuel to push you forward or is it draining you of all hope and positive energy? Are you proud to tell your story or somewhat embarrassed? This step is crucial because it forces you to think about the result. The only way to do this is to be honest with yourself by looking as clearly as possible at the outcomes you're experiencing. ***The*** *survivor narrative limits me because I am limited to my own actions and thoughts. No one else can contribute or interfere, and that's damaging for my progress. But I still can't let go of needing to feel in control.*

The fourth step is to reframe your story using new reference points. You are not telling yourself something that isn't true to make you feel better. When you change your narrative, it is not your life that you are changing; it is the way that you view it. It is still authentic, but your thinking is shifted so that you reframe the story under a new light. *I'm a survivor, but the time has passed that I need to remain only a survivor. Control is important, but it also is limiting in my life today. I can let go of control and things will still be fine. I will feel uncomfortable, but slowly things will prove to be okay. I did what was necessary in the past, and today I am in completely different circumstances.*

Following these four steps will help you identify your self-talk narrative and recognize what your emotional downfall is and what can change for greater resilience and calm. Think about what stories you are telling yourself and others about you. Are your personal narratives serving you or are you serving your personal narratives? Do you have the courage and tenacity to change your story if that is what's called for?

Beyond the personal narratives, there are a few ways to think about changing your general habits of negative self-talk that make you susceptible to emotional reactivity and instability.

The first step is awareness. If you are in a habit of negative self-talk, it is hard to change this to positive self-talk without being acutely and realistically aware of the thoughts that run through your mind. You can't stop interrupting people if you have no idea you are doing it. You may not even be aware of the times you say negative things to yourself because it may come as an automatic reaction.

Some common negative phrases may not even mean much to you, but their effect can be subtly profound. A common phrase is saying to yourself, "I can't." This is something that you may not even notice after a while, but every time you tell yourself you can't do something, it negates the possibility of even trying. Another phrase is "it's too difficult." For our purposes, healthier self-talk consists of avoiding phrases like "I'm so frustrated" and other negative emotions. These phrases can cause a mental block that will prevent you from being successful at a task simply because your mind has already decided that you've failed. When you say it, you live up to it for better or worse.

If you find yourself in one of these moments and with one of these thoughts, then work on contradicting or altering them, whether it is in your mind or out loud. Any time you think "I can't," immediately say, "But actually, I can." When you think "it's too difficult," immediately say, "But actually, it's not." When you think "I'm so frustrated," follow it up with, "But I'm fine now." If these become an automatic reaction to negative self-talk, then you will be able to mentally convince yourself of the positive thoughts instead of dwelling on the negative ones.

If you are in a situation where negative thoughts seem to bombard you and you don't know what to do, then stop again. Say to yourself, "What is my next step?" When faced with an actual question that needs an answer, you will be less preoccupied with your internal anxiety and more with how to manage the present. You cannot change the past, nor can you control the future. What you can do is take certain steps that allow you to predict the most probable future and be more comfortable with what can happen.

Imagine that you are doing a last-minute work project where something has gone wrong and you're not sure if you will finish. Your thoughts may be in a state of panic and anxiety. You aren't making much progress, and all you can think about are the mistakes that led you to that point. You begin to think, "I'll never be able to finish in time. I'm such a terrible student. I don't deserve good grades." This is the point where you must stop everything immediately and take a moment to assess your situation.

The first thing you should do is take the last thought you have and say, "Yes, I can," whether it is out loud or firmly in your mind. The next thing you need to do is ask yourself, "What can I do right now?" The answer to that is almost always very obvious. In this situation, it may just be that you need to do a bit more research, collate all your documents, and send them where they need to go. A good idea is to say the steps out loud or write them down somewhere where you can cross them off as they're done. A visual reminder of your progress is sometimes very important for your motivation.

By focusing not on what happened to get you in your situation and instead on what you can do to move forward, you will change your negative self-talk to positive courses of action. Blame and guilt are useless; steps to fix problems are far more helpful. Taking these steps requires you to focus your thoughts and inner talk on the here and now, which is the best way to dismiss negativity.

Finally, remember that feelings (and the negative self-talk they lead to) are not facts. The terrible and horrific ways you talk to yourself are a reflection not of reality, but of your emotions.

If you feel negatively about a certain person, they must be terrible. If you feel optimistically about a test, it must be easy. If you feel doubtful about a promise, the person on the other side of the promise must be scheming something. Emotions, both mild and intense, create an altered reality.

With negative self-talk, observed evidence of reality is discarded in favor of the truth of your feelings about the event. For that reason, our self-talk is one of the most dangerous obstacles to resilience because it can be so wildly different from reality and can change in the span of minutes. Is reality actually changing moment by moment? Of course not! Only the way you talk to yourself is changing that quickly.

Reality is neutral, and only you perceive it in any particular way. Viewing a situation with negative self-talk is like watching a completely benign scene with horror music being played over it. And then joyous music. And then the next minute, music fitting for a clown's entrance. Now compound this with the act that everyone has a different soundtrack playing over the same scene. You won't know what's really happening in front of your face because the music will influence you a certain way. The only hope you have is to *turn off the music*—by removing negative self-talk from the equation as best as you can.

This is a point to make sure you aren't being controlled by your negative or disempowering self-talk, which is not based on evidence or what's in front of you—it's based on past experiences, assumptions, or unfair associations. Feel your feelings—sometimes they are a signal for something that you don't consciously perceive, which is why they shouldn't be totally discounted—but don't become overwhelmed by them.

Takeaways:

- Our lowest emotional points don't exist in isolation; they almost all exist due to various cycles of triggers, emotional needs, behaviors, and then consequences—all of which strengthen the cycle for the future. So it's necessary to cut the cycle short and interrupt it in any way that we can. The most valuable way we can do this is through simply analyzing how it takes place in our lives.

- The first tool for this is the ABC Loop, which stands for antecedent, behavior, and consequence. They generally describe the main elements of an emotional outburst that we can break down and analyze: what happens before, what you did to cope, and what happens afterward that makes the cycle even harder to escape.

- The second tool is similar but more in-depth: emotional dashboarding. It describes the same cycle but through a different lens, with elements of situations, thoughts, emotions, bodily sensations, and impulses/actions. This gives you an even deeper view into certain situations and why you felt the need to lash out or become dragged down by negativity. The important thing to keep in mind with both of these tools is that the willingness for deep honesty is required.

- Finally, we come to a tool that underlies everything: self-talk. Most of the time, our self-talk is negative and disempowering. We may not even realize that our lens on the world and ourselves is negative because we've held this type of narrative about our lives for so long. But negative self-talk just makes you less resilient. The world is neutral, and our self-talk is what determines our emotions much of the time. Self-awareness is the key here; would you speak to a close friend like you speak to yourself?

Chapter 5. The Emotional Immune System

It's been mentioned that self-esteem is the emotional immune system, and for good reason. When self-esteem (and not ego) is present, it determines how you feel about yourself, your self-talk narratives, and your baseline of resilience. Someone who feels good about themselves is even-keeled and calm, even in the face of failure, because they know they are a three-dimensional being with lots of positive traits and skills.

And of course, if you have higher self-esteem, your emotional needs are already more satisfied. This means that fewer things will trigger you; or at least it will take more powerful triggers to affect you.

Let's start with low self-esteem, and then we can work our way to healthy self-esteem. This is the feeling that you aren't good enough, that you are inadequate, that you'll be judged by others, and that others will reject you for being who you are. It's a feeling of constant insecurity in yourself and being terrified that others will agree with you. Many of our emotional needs and insecurities stem from this point—that you are somehow "less" than others. This creates an inevitable dynamic where you are always seeking to be accepted and seen as "equal" to others.

An example of this is a study by Keiichi Onoda of Shimane University in Japan. His study found that when our self-esteem is low, we experience rejection as more viscerally painful than when our self-esteem is high. Because of this, we withdraw from others and our confidence is diminished. Having good self-esteem not only gives you feelings of higher self-confidence, but also means that you will better be able to cope with certain pressures—your internal monologue turns from "I can't do it" to "I can handle this."

Low self-esteem also makes us more vulnerable to failure. We experience greater drops in motivation and have less perseverance after suffering setbacks or failures than those with higher self-esteem. It can also make us more vulnerable to anxiety and stress. Worse still are the results from a study conducted by Lupis, Sabik, and Wolf from Brandeis University. They found those who have lower self-esteem release a higher amount of cortisol, the stress hormone, into their bloodstream when they experience stress, and it stays there for a longer period of time. Low self-esteem quite literally makes you less emotionally stable. It truly functions like our real biological immune systems.

Another study led by Jeff Greenberg of the University of Arizona examined how people dealt with the anticipation of receiving a mild electrical shock. Half of the participants received an intervention that was aimed to improve their self-esteem, while the other half did not. Though they believed they were going to get shocked, no electrical shock was actually administered; it was only the expectation of it that was important. The results were clear: those whose self-esteem was boosted showed significantly less anxiety than the others.

These findings all indicate that our self-esteem is responsible for not only our attitude and behaviors, but also the physiology of our bodies. Higher self-esteem means that common psychological problems such as rejection, failure, anxiety, and stress are easier to cope with. Therefore, boosting our self-esteem will have an immediate effect on our emotional resilience.

For better or worse, our self-esteem also tends to have a baseline.

This is a general set level to which it commonly returns and is where people's resilience is based. The higher your baseline, the higher your emotional resilience. However, though there is a baseline, self-esteem is unstable enough that it fluctuates daily, if not hourly. To make things more complicated, our self-esteem is made up of not only how we feel about ourselves generally, but also how we feel about ourselves in specific areas of our lives—for example, as a parent, student, musician, or friend.

The more meaningful one of these areas is to us, the greater its impact on our overall self-esteem. If you were a professional chef and someone doesn't like the taste of your cooking, this will affect your overall self-esteem much more than it would affect someone that doesn't think cooking is a major aspect of their identity. Similarly, if you pride yourself on being a good parent and trying to do the best for your children, criticisms toward your parenting skills will affect you much more than other criticisms you may receive.

The extent that something will affect you is all about how important an area is to your overall identity. Knowing this means that you can understand why you are being affected by something and that you can better control your reaction and your self-esteem in response. Instead of feeling your self-worth plummet because someone doesn't like your meal, you can identify that it is important to you and instead ask them how to improve. Identifying the problem means that you have something to fix instead of just generalizing and thinking that you will never be able to succeed because of one criticism.

Mind Games

An important factor is the need to be realistic and set correct expectations.

Self-esteem is useless if it is based upon a version of you that does not exist or no longer exists. Claiming that you were a certain weight in high school, that you could run so many miles when you were younger, or that you were once able to solve a particular calculus equation at one point in time isn't something that you need to dwell on. That's simply not who you are anymore, so always comparing yourself to that person is an exercise in futility.

You are different, and that's not necessarily negative. We all have skills that we pick up and lose as life goes on. Just because you used to be much better at something, or able to do it at all, doesn't mean you need to make comparisons to your past self. You may have lost some skills, but perhaps you've also gained some in the process. Today you may be a better cook than you ever were, a better writer, or more business-savvy than ever before.

For every skill or aspect you liked about your former self, another has taken its place that is equally praise-worthy. Don't sit around and reminisce about how you could once play the guitar really well. Value yourself on things that you are able to do right now. If it really means that much to you, you can very easily pick up the instrument and learn how to play again—most of us will never take this step, so it's clearly not that important to us and is used primarily to beat ourselves up via comparisons.

Evaluate yourself based on who you are at this very moment, not on some past version of yourself and not some future version that you believe you should be. Your self-image should change and adjust constantly to match who you are and who you've become, based on current abilities and skills. Adjust your beliefs about yourself so that they are realistic and focus on your current strengths, goals, and aspirations.

In this way, you will be accepting yourself for who you are, and your self-esteem will lift as a result. We are always told when we are younger to stop comparing ourselves to others because we are all different and all have different paths, goals, and decisions in life. By the same principle, we should stop comparing ourselves to who we used to be or who we think we should be. By accepting who we are right now, we will be infinitely more satisfied in all aspects of our lives.

This stands in stark contrast to the perfection myth that some people pursue and whose self-esteem suffers as a result. Myths of perfection come from unrealistic and too-harsh expectations of ourselves. Rationally, we know that nobody is perfect, but we still hold ourselves up to ideals that we may never be able to reach. Buying into these myths of what is and isn't acceptable will only hurt you and the other people in your life. You are just setting yourself up to be inevitably disappointed when you realize you won't reach perfection.

Reality will almost always clash with ideals of perfection, and this may lead to a dissatisfaction that can never be fixed. Perfection is simply unattainable for any of us. This is something we need to accept. You're never going to be absolutely perfect. You're never going to have the perfect body, the perfect life, the perfect relationship, the perfect children, or the perfect home. Even if you think you have a degree of perfection, there will always be someone with more of something or someone who is better at something.

Take hold of your accomplishments as you achieve them. Acknowledge them for their actual value. Stop devaluing your achievements by saying that you could have done better, that it wasn't entirely perfect, or even that it wasn't a big deal for you. Appreciate them for what they are: achievements in their own right.

It may help to keep a journal or a list of things that you accomplish each day as a reminder of all you can achieve. Everything from large triumphs to tiny victories. Not only will it lift your spirits when you have feelings of self-doubt, but it will inspire you to do more, just so you can write more. You may choose to write daily or maybe even once a week or month. It doesn't matter how you choose to take note of your accomplishments, just that you do. Because small goals are easy and quick to accomplish, you will build momentum each time you achieve something and then strive to keep going.

When something doesn't go perfectly, it's not a reflection of you. A key part of self-esteem is learning to differentiate between circumstances and your identity. Your circumstances are external events you may not have control over. You are not your mistakes. Your identity is not based on the last thing that you did or did not do successfully. It is more useful and effective to concentrate on things that you can change as opposed to things that you can't.

For example, perhaps you have decided you want to be more fit and healthy. You start eating healthy foods and exercising several times a week. You have changed your entire life around, banned all sugar from the house, and are only allowed healthy things. The problem is that one day you get a terrible craving and eat decadent chocolate cake instead of the healthy meal you were planning.

Before thoughts of failure kick in, or the feelings of inadequacy because you didn't successfully stick to your plan, take a moment to put things into perspective.

Making one bad eating decision is not fundamental to who you are as a person. It should only be treated as a mistake that you will try to rectify, not as a sin that will forever mean that you weren't good enough. Remember the rest of your victories over the week or month. Instead of focusing on one decision that doesn't define who you are, focus on the decision itself. Perhaps you might rework your diet so that on occasion you may have food you love in smaller quantities that won't affect your overall health.

The key here is to focus on how to improve, not on what you think you've done wrong by not reaching perfection. Your self-esteem will improve if you focus less on your perceived failures and more on trying to strive for success.

It's clear that boosting our self-esteem can improve our emotional immune system. But how do we do this when our self-esteem is low? Isn't that like telling a slow runner to simply run faster if they want to improve their running?

One of the keys is to pursue activities that remind you of your self-worth. Identify something you're good at; perhaps it's cooking or maybe it is a particular sport. Once you have that activity in mind, make sure you allocate time to actually engage in these activities. Self-esteem is built up when you achieve and improve in areas of your life that matter. If you pride yourself on being a good cook, throw more dinner parties and try to perfect difficult recipes. If you pride yourself on being a good runner, try for a new personal best, sign up for races or marathons, and train for them. Identify your core strengths (everyone has them, even you) and find opportunities and careers that allow you to capitalize on them.

By focusing on your strengths and successes, self-esteem that was once restricted to certain domains will begin to transfer to the rest of your life. This will allow you to work on your weaknesses in privacy and safety because you will be firm in the knowledge that it is your strengths that define you, not your weaknesses. When you feel good about what you can do, not what you can't, you can concentrate and remember these strengths in times of hardship.

Self-criticism is hard to ignore. We all want to be better and can't help but judge much of what we do too harshly, even if we wouldn't judge another for it. Even if it feels compelling or motivating, self-criticism is almost entirely useless. This is because you're focusing on the negative things instead of the positive. If your goal is to enhance your self-esteem, you need to substitute self-criticism with self-compassion.

To do this, any time your self-critical inner monologue kicks in, take a moment to consider the criticisms themselves. Imagine if a close friend was in the same situation. Would you have the same reaction? We tend to be far more compassionate to our friends than to ourselves. Think about what you would say to a friend in your situation and direct those comments at yourself instead. Doing so will avoid damaging your self-esteem further with critical thoughts. Instead, you will be able to build up your self-esteem and treat yourself less harshly as a result. This subtly speaks to the types of harsh and unrealistic (and perfectionistic) expectations you place on yourself and how damaging they are.

For example, imagine yourself trying to engage in a new hobby. Learning a new skill is always difficult, and you know this. However, you find yourself not showing even the slightest bit of improvement or success. Self-critical thoughts may begin at this point. It may not even be because you aren't very good at one particular activity. Often it may spiral into thoughts of every other thing that you may or may not be good at.

This is where you need to stop and take a step back. What would you say to a friend that was also struggling with one of their new activities? Chances are you'd probably say something much more positive, something about keeping motivation and practicing again and again until you succeed. You may feel like this is sugarcoating the issue a bit, but it's also the truth and not the worst possible interpretation of the events at hand.

Now direct that positivity at yourself and replace those negative self-critical thoughts you had before. You're only human and you're allowed to not be perfect. By giving yourself a chance to fail and by being okay with that failure, you're really giving yourself a chance to succeed and thus boosting your self-esteem.

The Self-Esteem Cycle

Why are some people able to roll with life's punches and come out on top while others feel so much less emotionally robust and able to cope with adversity?

Many people fundamentally misunderstand the nature of self-esteem and where it really comes from. We might think that a high self-esteem comes as a reward for being "good enough" or that it's a state of mind that occurs when external elements recognize our worth and praise or reward us.

But self-esteem is an *inner* quality that is wholly independent from the external, even though it interacts and adjusts with reality. High self-esteem is not arrogance, nor is it the feeling of being immune to criticism or as though one is perfect. Similarly, high self-esteem doesn't mean we never encounter doubt or difficulty in life.

Simply, self-esteem can be better thought of as a *how* rather than a *what*. The practice of self-esteem is an ongoing cycle of behaviors, processes, and attitudes that we can strengthen and cultivate in everyday life.

It's never just one thing that makes you feel bad about yourself, and likewise, it's never just one thing that makes you feel more secure in who you are. The best way to see this in action is to look at the process as it unfolds in a person with a low self-esteem and then to compare it to what it looks like in a person with a healthier self-esteem.

Element 1: At-risk situations

An at-risk situation is any set of circumstances that directly challenges and threatens your unhelpful assumptions, core beliefs, and "rules" about life. The key here is that these situations are distressing precisely because they challenge our maladaptive beliefs about ourselves.

Consider a student who has the core belief of "I am not good enough." This forms a cluster of unhelpful "rules" that he has to follow, such as "I have to perform perfectly at school" or "I can never fail."

These are self-imposed rules, and as long as they are followed, the student feels okay about himself. His feeling okay is not true self-esteem, however, because the underlying core belief is still there, only hidden in a situation that doesn't trigger it. Should a situation develop in which the rule is broken and the assumptions threatened, this false sense of self-esteem will crumble.

The student may do poorly on a particular test (understandable, since nobody is perfect!) and immediately breaks his own unhelpful rule. This puts him at risk of low self-esteem since it triggers the core belief of "I am not good enough."

Element 2: Activation of unhelpful core beliefs

Notice that it is not the situation itself that is inherently causing the distressing feelings, but activation of the student's internal core belief. Similarly, the student can't be said to have high self-esteem outside of an at-risk situation—it only looks that way because his core beliefs have not been activated.

Examples of unhelpful core beliefs that can be activated:

"I am useless."
"I'm a bad person."
"I'm stupid."
"I can't cope with life."

Element 3: Developing biased expectations

So certain situations threaten to undermine our corresponding "rules" and then our core beliefs become activated. What happens next? If the rule has been bent a little but not exactly broken (for example, doing okay on a test but not exactly excelling) you may then develop an expectation of how the situation will further develop. This expectation is *biased* in the sense that it heavily favors a negative interpretation, one that confirms your negative core belief. You start to assume the worst and jump to unpleasant conclusions about the situation's outcome, seeing catastrophe everywhere.

The student in our example may make "predictions" such as "I'm going to fail this whole course," "the teacher probably thinks I'm an idiot," or "I bet everyone else is going to do better than me this year."

These negative predictions then push him to behave in corresponding ways. Perhaps the student starts to feel defeated and sabotages his studies by not trying too hard on the next test—this is escaping behavior. He may start procrastinating on homework and simply avoid the looming deadlines he has—this is avoidance behavior. Alternatively, he might throw himself into over-studying, punishing himself with late nights—this is precaution-taking behavior.

Whichever route he goes for, though, they all leave him with a host of negative emotions. These negative emotions form a framework through which everything else is interpreted. But it can be a self-fulfilling prophecy: if anxiety about poor future performance actually damages those future performances, he might confirm the negative beliefs that led to that anxiety in the first place, creating a vicious cycle.

Without giving himself the chance to challenge these biased perceptions, they only become more and more concrete. He may "teach" himself to cling to escaping, avoidance, or precaution-taking behavior. Even when things turn out well, his biased expectations force him to interpret them badly. "I was lucky this time" or "this outcome was just a fluke; it doesn't mean anything."

Element 4: Developing negative self-evaluations

Alongside the building of biased expectations, he might simultaneously develop a negative perception of himself, especially if the "rule" he had was actually broken. If the student fails a test outright, he might be consumed with shame and self-criticism. Tried, judged, and executed in the court of his own mind, the student might berate himself and let those negative core beliefs run amok.

And just as with biased expectations, this inward assessment of his value as a human being causes certain harmful behaviors in response: retreating from life, self-harm, neglecting to take care of himself, giving up, or accepting poor treatment because he doesn't believe he deserves any better.

Element 5: Negative core belief is confirmed

By this point, low self-esteem is in full swing and may cause the student to feel depressed and extremely down about himself. Negative "self-talk" nurtures the harmful core beliefs, these beliefs bias expectations and self-evaluations, and these both cause the student to behave in ways that reinforce that core belief, starting the process over again. The belief is kept alive and current—"I'm not good enough"—even though the triggering event (doing poorly on an exam) has long since passed.

This is why so many people appear to have low self-esteem when they seem to outsiders to be doing well in life—the original negative life experiences have passed. The person is *actively maintaining* feelings of worthlessness in the present with their thoughts and corresponding actions.

So you can see that self-esteem is not a fixed state of mind, but rather a complex of interacting thoughts, feelings, and actions that reinforce a negative underlying belief that one is, essentially, "bad."

Knowing how this process works, and knowing that poor self-esteem begins with at-risk situations, we can take conscious control and deliberately work to reverse the cycle, curb negative self-talk, and begin to replace harmful core beliefs with more realistic, helpful ones.

Let's consider the same student who instead manages to halt the process of negative expectations and self-assessments. Let's look at how he might use knowledge of the model described above to foster a healthier, balanced state of mind when it comes to his studies.

Turning the low self-esteem cycle on its head

Again, imagine that the student does poorly on a test or fails it outright. These triggers threaten to undermine his "rules," and this then activates his core belief that he is not good enough. The experience of feeling his self-concept threatened in this way can serve as a flag for the student, alerting him that he is in a vulnerable position.

Here, he can pause and merely notice what he is feeling and thinking:

What emotion is looming on the horizon?
What thoughts and beliefs are behind this feeling?
What "rules" does he sense being broken or threatened here, and could this be activating a negative core belief?

A good way to get a handle on these processes is to write them down or keep a "thought diary." Take the time to notice when you are triggered and try to unpick thoughts and behaviors *before* they happen. Naturally, this is something that improves with practice.

Knowing how things could unfold, the student might choose to look more closely at his expectations and self-assessments. If he catches himself in self-talk that tells him how things are only going to end badly, he can recognize this and pin it down.

Is it strictly true that doing poorly on one test means you can't ever do well on another test again? Going deeper, is it really true that he has to perform perfectly every time, or else? Going even deeper still, is it really true that he is not good enough?

By slowing the process down and shining some conscious attention on these processes, the student can give himself time to stop them and adjust as necessary. Similarly, he can notice when he is making self-assessments that are fuelled by his negative core belief. He might write a mantra at the front of his notebook—"You are a good person. You don't have to be perfect"—and remind himself to read it again and again.

By changing his biased expectations and harmful self-evaluations, he gives himself the opportunity to then engage in behaviors that will help rather than hinder. Instead of withdrawing, avoiding, or taking precautions, he can take on his activities with an open, accepting mind and engage with new challenges with optimism. Without the baggage and momentum of low self-esteem, he can appraise each new situation afresh, approaching opportunities and trials without fear or resistance.

What's more, healthy behaviors like this will reinforce themselves with time, confirming a more helpful core belief—"I am a good person." Instead of getting caught in spirals of shame and self-blame, the student can recognize when he has behaved in adaptive, healthy ways. He can push himself to carry on studying and engaging with his schoolwork, despite his previous test result. When negative thoughts and feelings come up, he can use the opportunity to reexamine and gently challenge his expectations, interpretations, and core beliefs. And when he behaves in healthy ways, he can stop and take the time to notice and reward himself.

Did he do better on the next test? It would be a good idea to reward himself—not for doing well on the test, but for getting closer to a healthier core belief. New core beliefs will only strengthen the more we can acknowledge them as evidence for alternative beliefs. Remember to "bank" these gains and recognize them for the growth that they represent.

Nurturing self-esteem means continually pausing to question beliefs you may have just assumed to be correct in the past. If you discover a "rule," prediction, or assumption about the world or yourself, stop and take a close look at it.

- Is this really an accurate portrayal of reality?
- What are the pros and cons of thinking/feeling/acting this way, and do you want these results?
- What impact do these beliefs have on how you behave and feel?
- Is there a way to adapt these beliefs so they're more realistic and helpful?

Doing so then gives you the chance to reconsider the behaviors that come from these thoughts, beliefs, and feelings. If believing that you are incompetent means you never try anything, the outcome will be a self-fulfilling prophecy. But if you deliberately decide that the most helpful behavior will be to actively engage with life despite uncertainty, you put yourself on a different path.

Instead of setting yourself up for more of the same, you open to new opportunities and experiences. You become more flexible, more responsive to life, and better able to learn. You may or may not find yourself adjusting unhelpful rules and assumptions, but you at least give yourself the opportunity to question them, immediately empowering yourself and confirming your ability to take control of your own self-esteem. Every time you approach a new at-risk situation, you are strengthened and better able to cope.

Again, we can see that healthy self-esteem is not a single behavior or feeling but an ongoing series of feelings and behaviors. Individuals with healthy self-esteem

- have realistic expectations of themselves, others, and the world that are not overly biased
- have self-evaluations that are not filled with blame, condemnation, or judgment
- choose those behaviors that are most helpful and adaptive to them
- have core beliefs that are reasonable and open to adjustment with further evidence
- have rules and assumptions about life that do not result in negative self-evaluation or biased expectations

Overall, a person with high self-esteem can manage even challenging situations because they have unshakeable core beliefs that they are worthy. They do not make external circumstances a condition for their own self-acceptance.

A student with a healthy self-esteem is able to say, "I did poorly on this test. I'm not happy about it, but that's okay. I don't have to be perfect all the time. I'll try to understand what I didn't get right the first time around and will do my best on the next test. I trust myself to figure it out. Through challenges and difficulties, I'm still a good person. No matter what."

Takeaways:

- Self-esteem is the emotional immune system because it insulates you from emotional triggers, needs, and pains. The person who generally feels positively about themselves is not prone to emotional instability or reactivity because they simply aren't affected in the same way.
- Like the external world, our identities are entirely neutral, and self-esteem is a lens we view ourselves through. This means we have the power to see ourselves however we want, and for some of us, this is terrible news. A primary reason is an unreasonable set of expectations about yourself, the world, and your place in it—you will never live up to these expectations, so you can literally only fail in your mind, which makes you feel even worse than before.

- Self-esteem, as with many things about emotions, is not living in a vacuum and is best understood as a cycle of causes and effects. We begin with inaccurate assumptions and arbitrary (and disempowering) rules about life that are confirmed through inevitable failure. Then our narrative begins to include this data point and creates an increasingly negative self-evaluation. The inaccurate assumptions and beliefs are then strengthened, and it becomes even more difficult to climb out of this pit of despair. Deciphering these beliefs and seeing them nullified by reality is key.

Chapter 6. Philosophical Perspective

When we speak of the merits of "emotional toughness," the term might be misinterpreted as "coldness and distance" or, worse, "harshness and aggression." There are certainly cases in which efforts to maintain toughness have resulted in actions or statements that are aloof or abusive.

But the kind of resilience we're concerned with isn't something we direct toward others—it's about how we manage ourselves, how we rise to challenges or adversity, and how we persist. It doesn't harm our interpersonal relationships; in fact, it's something that actually improves how we connect and care for ourselves and others.

In this chapter, we'll discuss two similar ways to develop and refine emotional resilience. Both have roots that go back thousands of years, so the fact that we're still talking about them speaks to their lasting influence. One was popularized by the famed philosopher-emperor Marcus Aurelius of ancient Rome, while the other was developed by the one and only Buddha. Both deal with how we perceive the emotional substance of our realities and how regulating our feelings and temper is essential to experiencing a happy life. Additionally, they both work from the perspective of the "vast universe" and our tiny, insignificant place in that universe.

Detachment

"Attachment is the origin, the root of suffering; hence it is the cause of suffering."
—*The Dalai Lama, 1988*

The tenets of detachment are in the first known volumes of Buddhist thought, the

Pāli Canon. It's expressed as *nekkhamma*, which roughly translates to "renunciation." We often refer to this trait as "detachment," but it's perhaps more accurately expressed as "nonattachment."

Nonattachment isn't the same as deprivation. Consider food, for example: we have to eat to preserve ourselves, and there's nothing wrong with enjoying it. What nonattachment *does* address is desire and craving. It's logical to assume that when we cease dependence on certain life conditions, our odds of having a happier existence improve. We may still need it but don't feel emotionally empty without it.

Dependence on External Things

We pin our internal happiness to external people, objects, and circumstances because of the feelings they bring us. We're conditioned to be that way. Getting material goods and emotional satisfaction feeds an internal sense of completion. Once we obtain those things or satisfy those desires, we tend to cling to them for dear life. We fear losing them and stress out over that fear. We feel shattered if we lose something or grieve when a situation changes. Breaking up, getting laid off, and losing a house or a car are major, traumatic events.

Our attachment to these feelings defines us. We feel euphoria over positive results and devastation over negative ones. Strangely, we depend on *both* of those feelings, happy and sad, for our own comfort. Wallowing over regrets and disappointments can be a source of safety. The act of suffering can be as cozy and familiar as an easy chair. In trying to hold onto emotional habits, we restrict our ability to experience joy in the present.

When we stop trying to exercise control over the world around us, we actually set ourselves free. We give the world the freedom to fulfill us and remove its power to destroy us. Letting go is letting happiness *in*.

This isn't a quick fix or a one-time decision. It's a commitment that must be deliberately renewed day to day, moment to moment. That in itself is the opposite of instant gratification, which is always temporary. It's something that must be cultivated, not just granted. It's a change to the way you experience and interact with the things and feelings you want.

The Problems with Attachment

Claiming that our unhappiness or depression is caused by attachment may still seem contradictory. Isn't getting what we want a good thing? Doesn't it drive us to work harder to achieve a physical level of comfort? Doesn't it reinforce our values?

Attachment plays a role in the conflicts over daily issues and occasional events. For example, arguments with others arise from our strict attachment to our opinions. When something doesn't go our way, we get angry because of our attachment to the results we want. When we lose something we cherish, we feel sad because we're no longer attached to those objects. Our agony over losing a loved one comes from their attachment to our lives.

This isn't a criticism of the emotions we feel toward people or things. Love, enjoyment, intelligence, and comfort are not disorders or adverse conditions. Rather, we're discussing the reliance itself—the fact that our peace of mind *depends* on fulfilling those needs and our fixation on doing so.

Attachment to People

We may bristle at the suggestion that our attachment to *people* is an issue, but it's just as problematic. In fact, it could be *more* dangerous because humans are more unpredictable and susceptible to change. We're driven by nature, and nature changes all the time.

Attachment to others is a bred condition, not something that occurs overnight. We develop feelings by spending time with someone. With partners, we gain affection; with coworkers, we build cooperation; with friends and family, we gain enjoyment and sentiment.

But in all those situations, we're not really attaching to the people—we're attaching to the *experience.* Our connection is with the emotions we feel when we're with them, good or bad. Our mind identifies pleasant sensations, so we crave them more often. But as those attachments grow and deepen, we start to nurture discomfort and fear losing those pleasures. We believe our happiness rests with their presence, and that leads us to think we need an outside factor to be contented. By doing so, we forfeit our own power to make ourselves happy.

Connection versus Entanglement

Attachment puts us in a state of need. Everything we do and think is focused on the thing we're attached to. Our perspective blurs, and our connections with others turn into entanglements.

When we experience connection, we share bonds and commonalities but maintain our individuality. Our overattachment to the feelings we experience can distort that connection into codependency. We start thinking in terms of demands or needs. That's when we stop feeling connected and begin feeling *entangled*.

This is when we perceive external forces as things we need to be happy. But nothing outside of us can truly bring happiness or security. The only ones in control of our own happiness are ourselves—our dependence on others might obscure that fact, but it doesn't change it.

As our attachments grow, our expectations become more fixed in our minds. Our fear of losing what we desire becomes more acute. We become concerned that the person or thing we're attached to may fall short of our needs, if it is not lost altogether. The experience can be painful.

When that worry manifests, our mind puts us in "survival mode." We become focused, obsessed, and maybe even addicted to the objects of our attachment. We become clingy, controlling, domineering, and insecure. Such emotions lead to near-dysfunction and disrupt our balance, and we act irrationally.

Pain and Suffering Is a Choice

We choose to experience misery and hurt. Believe it or not, that's good news. We can avoid entanglement by living with nonattachment. That doesn't mean we withdraw or isolate ourselves from others and never connect with anyone again. It doesn't mean we sacrifice our dreams or aspirations. It doesn't mean we devalue love, support, association, or compassion.

What it *does* mean is that we release our *need* for the relationship or thing that we've become attached to. We accept things as they are and recognize that the situations in our existence will constantly evolve and change. Permanence is illusory—everything is temporary.

Accepting this viewpoint isn't automatic or easy. It requires letting go of details we feel strongly about but can't control. It's tough because our egos are constantly fed by the drive to *keep* that control. Releasing that need and putting our trust in the universe is a tough task. But the reality is that we really have no choice in what happens in our lives. We can either fight it or embrace it. When we detach, we embrace anything that comes, and we make the choice to find happiness in any situation.

Breaking Attachment

Detachment can be frightening, but it's much easier than it sounds. We don't just disengage with people or things—we merely change how we relate to them. Nobody feels *glad* about being dependent. Even if we claim to be happy, circumstances or events will arise that will expose that happiness as a fraud. Dependence only feels good when everything's going in our favor. When conditions change, or when people leave, that dependence becomes a source of anxiety.

Detachment relieves us of our expectations. Our happiness isn't based on need; it becomes authentic. We don't rely on things outside us to make us happy because we're complete as we are. We can achieve happiness on our own. Happiness from outside factors becomes an *addition* to our positive state of mind, not the only source for it. The following steps can help you develop a healthy detachment that will inform and reinforce your life and relationships.

Awareness. Look at the attachments you have in your life—your partner, your surroundings, your social circles, or your work. Where have you given up power? Do you expect something from those relationships or things? Is any part of your connection controlled by your fear, anxiety, or insecurity? Find out which situations you might need to detach from.

Examination. Now that you've identified these attachments, inspect them more closely. What fuels your attachment? Do fear or insecurity play a part? How valid are your fears? If you sense they're irrational, then what are you *really* worried about? Take a lot of time with this step.

Acceptance. Accept each moment exactly for what it is. Don't compare or try to turn it into yesterday—that's gone. Don't try to extend the moment into something that will last forever, because it won't. Absorb the moment fully and enjoy it, because it will pass.

Now is enough. Tomorrow will never be the same as today. Relationships will end; others will begin. Your surroundings will change. You'll be able to deal with those changes when they come. But right now, in the present moment, appreciate and enjoy what you have. No matter what the future holds, what you have now will always be enough.

Practice letting things be. Make peace with the moment. Don't worry if something's wrong with you or your life. Operate from a standpoint of acceptance.

This doesn't mean you can't work toward creating a better tomorrow or improving yourself. It just means accepting where you are now as the foundation for your achievements.

Release the need to know. Life will always be uncertain. Obsessing about tomorrow is self-defeating; there will always be another tomorrow after it. You can make projections and predictions about the future, and you might be right. But you can't affect them until they happen. The best way to be prepared is to work on what's before you right now.

If conventional Buddhist thoughts on detaching can be briefly summed up, it's about recognizing that everything good and bad in this world fades as quickly as it comes. We have no choice or control in it either way. Thus, we cannot expect what we want to happen, no matter how reasonable it is. The moment we form an expectation, we form an attachment to an outcome, and that makes you vulnerable to suffering (and emotionality). You can struggle and still receive a negative outcome, or you can embrace it as it comes.

Reinterpret Neutrality

Buddhist detachment can be difficult to wrap your mind around, but the essential idea is very similar to that of Stoicism. Stoicism is a way of viewing life and seeing your place in the world, and it was originally put into words by the Athenian philosopher Zeno around the third century BCE.

Stoic philosophy argues that unchecked emotions are some of the biggest enemies of your happiness and fulfillment. Rationality, perspective, and practicality are what drive Stoicism.

According to Stoicism, you have the utmost free will in any circumstance, regardless of what your emotions might tell you. There is your *emotional* reality and the *objective* reality, and you can choose which you want to abide by. You have more control of what's going on in your life than you realize.

Actually, you can choose the emotions you feel.

There are many ways to characterize Stoicism, but I find it best to break it into two primary tenets.

The first important tenet of Stoicism that will seek to promote emotional resilience is that everything that happens in the world is neutral—every event and consequence thereof. Every event has a different effect on everyone, but the events themselves are neutral, without intent, and play no favorites. There is no bad or good; it is all subjective. It is created with you, along with all emotions and judgments.

This means that it's your reaction and perception that cause your unhappiness. If you perceive events to be negative, they will be negative. If you perceive them to be positive, you will find the positive in them.

If you are sitting in a café and a car slams into your parked car on the street outside, you have a choice about how you will respond. It's a neutral event, and you can attach any set of emotions to it you want.

You can react the way most people do and freak out or play the victim, or you can calmly take out your phone and solve the problem by researching new cars with upgraded sound systems. The operative facts are the same, yet two very different outcomes will ensue. Which reaction do you think will lead to a more orderly resolution of what just happened?

No matter how you react, the facts will remain the same: your car is going to need repairs or will need to be replaced.

Your emotional stability hinges upon your reaction and perception of neutral events, and every event is neutral. It's your response and opinion about the event that either causes you tremendous emotional distress or leads you to a quick resolution with minimal stress. Taking ownership of your role in your level of happiness and stability is why the same event can affect people in drastically different ways.

What makes things negative, unpleasant, and stressful is our judgment of those otherwise neutral events. We don't have control over most of the situations we are put into, despite our best efforts. You can't control other people or the weather—if you feel that you do, you are fighting a losing battle because you are setting yourself up for continual disappointment. But we do have control over 100% of our reactions and responses to those situations. This is a process that can make or break your mood and perception of life.

People react in predictable ways when things they perceive to be negative happen. They either blame someone else, or they beat themselves up emotionally. Because of that lack of control over events, many are frustrated by their feelings of helplessness. Focus instead on how you respond to what's taking place right now in your life.

Outside forces are not out to make you miserable. Even if they are, you are making the choice to feel that emotion. Look within.

The world hands us a blank slate every morning; you are the sole writer and editor of what is written on that slate. Some people will inevitably see the silver lining of a storm cloud, while others are overwhelmed by the smallest hint of darkness. Which will you be?

"If you are pained by any external thing, it is not this thing that disturbs you, but your own judgment about it. And it is in your power to wipe out this judgment now."
– Marcus Aurelius

The second tenet of Stoicism is to always temper your expectations and expect difficulty and challenge. This isn't necessarily about being pessimistic; it's more about being realistic and steeling yourself for the hardships you'll encounter. It's amazing what adjusted expectations can do for your outlook: how would you feel if you won the lottery and expected to win versus if you won the lottery and forgot you had even bought a ticket?

Many of us are waking up with the former expectation—that life will or should deliver us something. It's a dangerous place to be. When you can move away from this thinking and ask yourself, "What's the worst that can happen?" you'll be prepared and unsurprised. Imagine yourself suffering, think about your death, and even practice a degree of abstinence of deprivation in your life. How will you feel afterward? As you may have surmised, Stoicism is a particularly helpful tool in battling the obstacles we face in our lives.

Going a step further, you can, as the Stoics say, *turn the obstacle upside down*. Train yourself to avoid judging events as purely good or bad. In fact, realize you can even turn all obstacles upside down, looked at through another perspective, to suit your purposes. This means that anything that seems to present an obstacle should actually be seen as an opportunity for something positive and growth-oriented. Remember, it is your interpretation of entirely neutral events.

So look at what happens objectively and dispassionately—it might be raining. And then choose your best reaction. The world won't end, and the activities you had planned for outdoors can be done another day. How might the rain force you to get creative or explore other untapped potential? What are the alternate perspectives you can adopt, rather than one of sadness or frustration? These alternate perspectives always exist, and you should train your ability to see them.

The truth is that you always have the ability to respond in a way that amounts to rolling with the punches. How might this obstacle become an opportunity, if only an opportunity to practice your sense of resilience and patience?

The most practical effect is enabling the sufferer (so to speak) to become immune to negative emotional spirals. Instead, they force themselves to engage in alternative thought patterns to gain perspective and move forward rationally. For example, imagine you are a nurse and you have a patient who is very cranky. The reason you approached this person is because you wanted to help them. But this person is being surly, doesn't want to cooperate, or even tries to bully you. In short, this person is being mean and nasty.

According to Stoics, instead of feeling hassled or feeling that this person is making your life difficult, try to think of this person as actually helping you out. How can that be? Well, this person's behavior is giving you a tremendous opportunity to exercise new virtues that you should have more of in your life, like being understanding, patient, and compassionate.

Another example drawn from Stoic teachings is the death of a loved one. If you love somebody, it's easy to fall into despair when they pass away. But you could use this loss as an opportunity to show fortitude. Instead of feeling pain and loss, you can look at this commonly negative situation as an opportunity to practice inner strength, calm, control, equanimity, and level-headedness.

Our life is full of teachable moments, like the parables of old or Aesop's Fables. Regardless of how negative a particular event may seem, you can always try to reinterpret it as a positive opportunity or look at the other side of the situation. The more you turn the obstacle upside down, the more you'll realize that there really is no such thing as good and bad. It all depends on how you choose to perceive something.

For centuries, Stoicism has been a virtual antidote for emotional disruptions that can plague any of us. It tells you that you unequivocally have the power to create your own reality. Meanwhile, Buddhist principles also make it clear that your surroundings don't need to change for change to occur. Your mental states are freer than you think, and sometimes a mental switch is all it takes for resilience to spring forth.

Takeaways:

- Sometimes a shift in perspective is all that is needed for something to finally click inside you. At the very least, we can combine these new perspectives with the techniques and tools we've learned to make you emotionally bulletproof.
- Here, we cover two of the world's oldest philosophies in dealing with hardship and optimizing for happiness. Buddhism is all about understanding that we cause our own suffering through attachment to people, things, outcomes, and thoughts. Everything is impermanent, and good and bad come and go like waves on the ocean. When we form an attachment, we form an expectation, which puts us in a position to tumble and fall. Thus, we must detach from the notion that external things or people are necessary for our happiness. In this way, we make ourselves entirely responsible for our state of mind.
- Stoicism has some philosophical overlap with Buddhism, but the emphasis is on what we can and cannot control. We cannot control anything in this world but our actions and thoughts, so we

must condition our happiness to depend happiness on those things. To do otherwise would be to remove all power from us. The world is a neutral place, and we can interpret it however we want; we only have to choose a favorable interpretation. In Stoicism, we must also turn the obstacle upside down and not see negative events as tragedy, but rather interpret and reframe them as learning experiences.

Chapter 7. Preventative Care

As we've discussed and you have no doubt noticed from your own life, the brain maintains a strong negativity bias.

Our continued survival depends on our ability to keep harmful elements at bay as much as possible—dangerous encounters, food one is allergic to, toxic people or situations to avoid, and so forth. But because neural activity in response to negative signals is so strong, it can cease being an effective survival mechanism and become an obstacle to your emotional stability and overall happiness.

We've gone over many techniques and tools for keeping it together and even-keeled in the face of emotional triggers and feelings of impending doom, but what about the everyday ways in which this negativity bias affects us? Part of the battle in staying even with your emotions is to actively battle this instinct and generate your own positivity.

To a lot of us, that's no small task. Negativity is more accumulative than positivity, piling up in the psyche with seemingly little effort. It's easy for the brain to lie back and let fears, terrors, and anxieties unfold one after the other. When they get to a certain mass, negativity bias starts to feel like an anchor that can't be overcome.

We tend to characterize positivity as something that requires more labor, an exhaustive act that might not even make a significant dent in our negativity in the end. But in reality, positivity is a force that pays off even when we take small steps to bring it about. It's far easier to inject positivity into our lives and emotions than our negativity would have us think.

Improving your emotional response and coping mechanisms will always be effective. But for everyday life, it's best to have some strategies that aren't necessarily developed in crisis mode. Taking preventative measures will keep you healthy and grounded and form a solid foundation that eases the strain of emergencies.

Be Grateful and Savor

We associate the emotion of gratitude with thankfulness for whatever comes into our lives, positive or not. Although the adage of being grateful for what we have is well-known, it's not always a practice we grasp, even though there's *always* something to be grateful for. Still, studies have shown that just being aware of or questioning your gratitude—even if you can't think of anything off the top of your head—can create some powerful chemical changes.

For example, stop reading for a minute and consider five things you're grateful for.

They don't need to be big accomplishments or achievements; they can be simple parts of everyday living. "I have clean air to breathe," "I have family and friends who love me," "I have a place to sleep," "I live in interesting times."

Now compare this to the everyday life of someone in abject poverty who's struggling to make ends meet and is on the brink of starvation. Or consider the tale of a ballet dancer who had to have her feet amputated (or something similarly morbid and unfortunate).

You might not have noticed any immediate changes, but a feeling of acceptance and perspective probably just entered your mind. You may not have everything that you want (none of us ever do), but your life is still pretty darn good. And it's been scientifically proven that gratitude is more or less a natural antidepressant. Thinking about or asking what you're grateful for actually activates certain neural circuits that produce dopamine and serotonin, the neurotransmitters that regulate our pleasure centers and mood levels. They then travel the neural pathways to the "bliss" center of the brain, much like a prescribed antidepressant. The more you stimulate them, the stronger and more automatic they become, and the more your resilience and calm become a natural way of living.

Hebb's law states, "Neurons that fire together wire together." We see this proverb at work in everyday life. When you're walking through a forest for the first time, you're forging a new path that can provide challenges. But the more the path is traveled, the more defined and easier to follow it becomes.

So it works with the human brain. The more a neural pathway is activated, the less effort it takes to animate it the next time. Since the practice of mental gratitude greases the neurons, simple, short daily meditations on your appreciation can actually ease your tension on a biological level.

Dopamine, in particular, is extraordinarily useful in attitude enhancement. It's called the "reward" neurotransmitter because it feels good to get. But it also helps initiate action, and increasing it makes you more likely to do whatever made you happier. It's like the brain saying, "That thing you just did? Yeah, do that again!"

The downside is that negative thought patterns activate *their* neural pathways as well. When we constantly see the negative aspects of a situation and seek out problems, the neural paths for negative thinking grow stronger. Proactively applying gratitude can train our brains to seek out constructive elements in our lives while lessening the destructive ones. We water the flowers instead of watering the weeds.

Researchers Robert A. Emmons and Michael E. McCullough performed a study in 2003 called "Counting Blessings Versus Burdens: An Experimental Investigation of Gratitude and Subjective Well-Being in Daily Life." They gathered a group of young adults and told them to keep journals. One group was instructed to write daily entries of things they were grateful for, and the other was told to write about their annoyances or why they were better off than other people.

The researchers' instructions to the gratitude journalists encouraged them to note any facet of their lives that they were grateful for, regardless of importance: "There are many things in our lives, both large and small, that we might be grateful about. Think back over the past week and write down on the lines below up to five things in your life that you are grateful or thankful for."

For journalists who were given the task of writing down their annoyances, the researchers said, "Hassles are irritants—things that annoy or bother you. They occur in various domains of life, including relationships, work, school, housing, finances, health, and so forth. Think back over today and, on the lines below, list up to five hassles that occurred in your life." The results were predictably persuasive. The gratitude journalists showed greater increases in determination, attention, enthusiasm, and energy. Their findings showed gratitude to be a powerful social and spiritual accelerator:

> The experience of gratitude, and the actions stimulated by it, build and strengthen social bonds and friendships. Moreover, encouraging people to focus on the benefits they have received from others leads them to feel loved and cared for by others... Therefore, gratitude appears to build friendships and other social bonds. These are social resources because, in times of need, these social bonds are wellsprings to be tapped for the provision of social support. Gratitude, thus, is a form of love, a consequence of an already formed attachment as well as a precipitating condition for the formation of new affectional bonds... Gratitude is also likely to build and strengthen a sense of spirituality, given the strong historical association between

gratitude and religion... Finally, to the extent that gratitude, like other positive emotions, broadens the scope of cognition and enables flexible and creative thinking, it also facilitates coping with stress and adversity.

Just as tellingly, the study proved that realizing that other people were worse off does *not* equal gratitude. Rather, gratitude is an appreciation of the positive aspects of your own situation.

Emmons and McCullough's findings could inspire you to try journaling yourself. Putting your thoughts in writing is almost always a good practice.

Start out by replicating the exercise at the beginning of this chapter: write down five things that you're grateful for. Make a conscious effort to reflect upon the things that bring you joy, elation, or peace of mind. As we've said, there's *always* something to be thankful for in a given situation. It might bring you additional perspective to write five things you have that most people do *not* have. Sometimes it's only through contrast that we can truly keep gratitude in mind.

Commit to this practice every day for the next 10 days. Keep a journal by your bed and take a minute before sleeping to recall the events of the day that made you smile. Or start a list on your smartphone to write pleasant events down as they happen (also a nice way for a quick pick-me-up when you're not having a great day). You can also find an "accountability partner" to keep a list like yours. Every week, you can check in for five minutes and read your lists to each other.

This practice can turn gratitude into your own mental gym—strength training for your neural pathways. The more you practice the act of gratitude, the healthier that muscle gets. Just like in physical gyms, the more you show up and work the gratitude angle, the easier the workouts get.

If writing feels like too much, you can ease into gratitude practice with an extremely uncomplicated daily exercise: every time your feet hit the ground after you get out of bed, simply say thank you. Nature likes to be appreciated and paid attention to in the same way that humans do. Acknowledging nature helps our own lives bloom in response.

We get used to whatever situations surround us without much effort. Initiating gratitude in all walks of our own lives might be a more trying task or even impractical in certain situations. When was the last time you turned the key in your car's ignition and praised the miracles of the internal combustion engine? Have you ever taken a walk through a city park and expressed thanks for arch supports? Do you take time from work to appreciate the craft and convenience of your hole punch or stapler?

But in truth, those are all perfectly fine things to be grateful for—especially when we don't have them. Natural disasters like hurricanes or earthquakes can give affected people a new appreciation for things like running water and electricity. It's true that nothing should be taken for granted—but realistically, that feeling doesn't necessarily last for long. A few days removed from those disasters, you're back to cursing the elevator if it takes more than 30 seconds to get to your floor.

The central point is that gratitude is easy to execute but not always easy to maintain. There's nothing wrong about expressing annoyances over little inconveniences, but letting those irritations inform the core of our beings is ill-advised. We've seen how our brain transforms itself based on even our smallest impulses. If we can make gratitude a more constant and consistent impulse, our brains will see to it that our happiness improves.

Studies have also been conducted to understand the benefits of *savoring*—the mental and emotional act of appreciating a particular experience while you are currently engaging in it. It can be said to be gratitude in real-time.

One such study investigated a group of depressed participants who were asked to take their time and relish an activity they normally hurry to get through. The activities were all part of their daily functions: eating a meal, taking a shower, finishing a work assignment, or walking to a subway or bus stop. The subjects were told to write down how they felt after extending these routines and how those feelings compared to those when they rushed through them.

Another study surveyed members of a community who were comparatively healthy in their states of mind. These participants were told to savor two pleasant experiences each day, simply by reflecting on them for two to three minutes and trying to make the pleasure last as long and intensely as possible.

The results for both studies were dramatic: taking time to savor certain events, even ones normally associated with routine and tasks, increased the participants' overall happiness and decreased their depression to some extent. The simple act of slowing down and being intentional with their actions improved how they felt about, well, everything.

The Journal of Positive Psychology noted that these and other findings supported the theory that "savoring responses is an important mechanism by which individuals transmute the raw stuff of daily life into positive effect." In other words, savoring in itself is a pleasurable activity. Savoring is a way to add and reinforce another layer of emotional benefit to an act of pleasure on top of the sensual and mental enjoyment that such acts provide.

Taking time to finish and appreciate a meal or dessert is an obvious example of physical savoring, but it's not the only one. Focusing, even meditating, on the character and nature of things we do and see ramps up the benefits as well. Viewing human drama from a park bench, experiencing the rush of breeze and motion in a bike ride, noting the give and take in a group conversation with friends—all are activities that can be transformed by stretching them out and appreciating each part. In reality, savoring is the act of stepping outside of your brain and anxieties and putting your focus onto a single, pleasurable thing.

Reflecting and communicating our appreciation of these experiences is another way to savor them after the fact. Whether one writes their thoughts down in a blog, talks about their experience to friends, or merely meditates and gives thanks privately adds another, deeper level to the episodes that make up our lives. The act of savoring can lead to a more conscious state of mind in which we have clearer, sharper interactions with the world and find more to appreciate about it.

Write It Out

Keeping journals is a part of almost any facet of modern life you can think of—business, art, information-gathering, and of course news. It's not a stretch to understand its service in the maintenance of ourselves and our mental health—we've already covered how it can help you bring awareness to your gratitude and savoring practices. A couple more journal techniques are particularly helpful in your quest for emotional calm.

"Worry journals" are an element of cognitive behavior therapy (CBT), a long-time aid in treating emotional disorders. They've also been used in sleep therapy for subjects who experienced anxiety. The goal of the worry journal is to air out our worries, fears, anxieties, and issues on paper throughout the course of the day.

One method of worry journaling involves writing one's concerns or fears on the left-hand side of a page, thinking about how to resolve them, and writing these plans on the right-hand side. The writer then closes the journal and at least tries not to think about the worries until the next day when, theoretically, some of the plans can be executed.

Researchers from Pennsylvania State University decided to see whether worry journaling alone could improve the emotional balance of subjects. They recruited 51 patients with various forms of anxiety disorder. From this pool, certain subjects were randomly selected to keep a worry journal for 10 days. Those remaining were told to keep a journal in which they simply recorded their thoughts. The researchers also text-messaged participants at random times during the day, prompting them to write immediately.

After the 10-day experiment ended, those with worry journals were asked to review how many of their worries had actually come true. Most of them (91%) hadn't. The brief text interventions were enough to significantly reduce their anxiety levels, more so than those who had simply kept thought journals. Thirty days after the experiment concluded, the worry journal group was still performing better than the control group.

An interesting finding of the Penn State study was how quickly the worry journal participants manifested positive changes, even after only 10 days. By documenting their worries, fears, obstacles, and predictions, they made progress in reorienting themselves to the present—not the future, where some of their biggest anxieties lay. There appeared to be a light at the end of the tunnel, and people weren't just spiraling into the worst-case scenarios. "It may also make the worthlessness of engaging in excessive catastrophic expectations more apparent," the researchers said.

These results support the idea that putting our self-inventories on record can be effective in managing stress. Worry journaling could be a beneficial part of your regular response to stress and daily routine. For example, let's say that your business has lost its biggest customer or that you've had a contentious argument with an employee. In frustration, you walk into your office and shut the door. Your emotions aren't controllable—you're upset, angry, and maybe even frightened of the fallout.

To regain your emotional balance, you focus on your breathing for a few moments. Then you open your journal. You write down exactly what's upsetting you, what you're worried about, and what your biggest obstacles, problems, or fears are. You must be honest—understand that nobody except you will read this journal unless you give it to them.

Some experts suggest writing in your journal every single day. That's certainly not a bad idea, but sometimes life intrudes upon our ability to do that. We don't always have time. Other days, we *do* have time but don't feel like we have anything significant to say. But in moments of worry, anxiety, or upset, we *always* have something to say— and plenty of it. Keeping it bottled up may prevent us from doing anything else until we finally express our frustrations, so that's a good reason to write it down in the journal on the spot.

These situations illustrate a good practice when it comes to journaling: *follow your emotional prompts.* Writing during times when we're scared, angry, or upset might not be the first action you'll think of taking, but it can go a long way in addressing your immediate emotional needs. By the time you're done, you might be at least a little glad you did, and chances are good that the next time, writing *will* be the first action you take.

The journal is where you dump your frustrations, problems, and concerns. Keep writing until you've finally written everything you need to say. Remember, the journal's a "safe zone" and you're not obligated to share it with anyone. It's where you can be direct, unsparing, and honest, without unforeseeable repercussions. Once you express these feelings and get them out of your system, you no longer feel that you are burdened by them internally.

Two outcomes will probably emerge from documenting your feelings. While writing, you'll gradually become calmer and less upset. You may start to see solutions to your problems come forth. Laying your problem out in words on the page makes a future course of action appear and helps you figure out what to do.

Journaling is free-flowing and open-ended, but another approach that could be helpful involves making two lists that are very specific in what they accomplish.

"Stop" and "It's Okay To" lists serve as daily affirmations of your values. They remind you what's acceptable and what's not, what boundaries you have set up, and what brings you closer to your goals. They're also empowering—they give you self-generated, unequivocal directions. "Stop" items are things you should hold yourself back from; "It's Okay To" items list out what's acceptable.

Write out these lists and post them in a place you see regularly. They'll serve as guidelines that will keep you on course to a life of emotional strength and wellness. See the following example:

STOP:	IT'S OKAY TO:
Putting yourself last	Ask people for help
Trying to be all things to all people	Be constantly changing
Being afraid to say no or yes	Admit vulnerability and weakness
Talking down to yourself	Not be impenetrable
Talking and not listening	Be knocked down and feel hopeless
Depending on others to make you happy	Cry
Letting outside events define you	Speak up for what you value
Settling for less	Take time to determine your feelings about a situation
Limiting beliefs	Always be in "learning" mode
Keeping score in games you don't need to—or can't—win	Question the rules of the games you do play

After making these lists, we can incorporate their contents into internal action when we have a conflict. Since they are based on the values *we* define for ourselves, the hope is that these principles will be easier to stick to when such a situation arises.

For example, someone in your extended family comes to you with an investment opportunity. They've had a difficult time staying afloat as an adult and have been bailed out once or twice after making some unwise credit decisions. You mistrust their judgment about financial matters. But since they're family, you let them talk to you, and you listen completely to their pitch.

While they seem earnest about the opportunity, you have doubts that it's anything more than a pyramid scheme, and you say so. The family member becomes angry and accuses you of being closed off to new ideas and "going against the family." You attempt to explain your position more patiently, but before you finish, they angrily stomp out. As a result, you feel some amount of guilt and shame.

Let's use the above "Stop/It's Okay To" lists to back up your reactions (your personal lists may be different, but for this example, we'll use ours). Your instincts told you to reject your family member's latest plan, and they responded negatively. One of the "Stop" items was "Being afraid to say no." Perhaps you have a tendency to help as many of your friends or family as you can, which is impossible to fulfill. But another "Stop" item is "Trying to be all things to all people." In this scenario, you've successfully prevented those acts from happening.

What about the "It's Okay To" list? You explained your reasons for not agreeing to invest in a patient manner. That could answer a couple of items on the "It's Okay To" list: "Speak up for what you value" and possibly "Take time to determine your feelings about a situation." You explained why taking on this dubious investment goes against your needs and principles, but only after you also let them finish so you could hear them fairly.

After the conflict ended, you might have felt guilty or ashamed. But you acted according to the ground rules you set forth in that list, which are completely reasonable and came from your own self-questioning. Knowing that you stuck to your own self-defined principles may not make you feel better *immediately*—but probably much sooner than you would have if you *didn't* stick to them.

Again, your personal list will likely vary from our example. You should have some items unique to your own experience, and that's what makes the lists invaluable. Mistakes, regrets, and even accidents can happen when we forget or work against our belief systems and values. These lists are one way to keep them near the forefront of our attention, and though they won't eradicate all conflict from our lives, they could help us navigate them with more assurance.

Stay in the Present

Mindfulness is "the practice of purposefully focusing all of your attention on the current moment and accepting it without judgment."

As a preventative measure, it doesn't get any better than this. It can keep your mind from overthinking and running amuck, which is the precursor to an emotional outburst. The person who is aware of their thoughts as they are happening is far more likely to keep it together versus the person who is unaware of what is happening in the present.

We've all been caught in our own thoughts—at one time or another—but how we handle those thoughts can make all the difference. Anxiety plays a key part in this by weighing down your brain—with the same old things. In doing so, you may find yourself feeling exhausted—and trapped within a mind loop—and unable to get free from thoughts of either the future or the past. Fortunately, focusing your attention on the present moment, rather than the what-ifs of life, can help you spend a lot less time being overwhelmed by worst-case scenarios.

For those who struggle with mindfulness, they may find themselves residing in a state of imagined consequences. If you ruminate, the event may not have even taken place, yet the worry in your head automatically draws you to it. However, when you begin to put mindfulness into practice, overthinking can eventually become a thing of the past, with both time and dedication.

Mindfulness will not only improve your concentration but also your physical well-being. In fact, some health-related issues are directly linked to a lack of sleep, so the sooner you can master your mental health, the sooner you can master your overall health. Mindful meditation can help make this so by increasing your relaxation response.

In a society that never stops, stress is inevitable. No matter the factor—whether it be work, school, family, friends, finances, and so on—stress can be debilitating. However, it's become so common that very few people know what action to take to rid themselves of its negative effects. In fact, many fail to realize how the severity of their stress can cause a plethora of health problems for them later on down the road.

But by taking part in mindfulness you can work your way back to emotional stability—instead of feeling pressured by the world around you. Once you've alleviated your stress at its source, you'll experience a great sense of peace throughout your day-to-day life while improving your overall mental health. Mastering mindfulness can be the start of a brand-new life, serving as your shield of protection for all things difficult—and allowing you to sidestep any conflict that tries to come your way.

Although practiced for thousands of years—by several groups of people—mindfulness was first introduced in the U.S. by Jon Kabat-Zinn. Mindfulness is something he'd learned himself while studying at MIT. The only difference is that he adapted its teaching to center around his own form—which strives to eliminate problem areas, such as stress. Yet while Hinduism, Buddhism, and other religions all embrace mindfulness, Kabat-Zinn strives to make mindfulness mainstream day by day by introducing it to a variety of individuals.

Everyone has a special place to call their own—which is extremely important when engaging in mindful meditation. In order to get the most out of your time, it is important that you find a spot that has a limited amount of distraction. In doing so, you are better able to focus on the task at hand—and work on freeing your mind—without interruption.

It's even more important to stick to a set routine. In turn, decide on a time that best works for you—when you are isolated, away from others, and free from business. This can help you be all the more determined—when first starting—so that you can be that much closer to a stress-free mind.

The two worst things you can do for yourself are focusing on past events that you can't change or focusing on present events and comparing them with your future. One is long gone, and one has yet to happen. Neither should be your concern.

That's why it's better that you focus on the here and now rather than to dwell on past situations like your very first heartbreak, first embarrassing moment, and so on; the same goes for future events. Then, as you begin to focus solely on the present, you'll find that it becomes a whole lot easier to center yourself with your mind, as well as with your environment.

Oftentimes, we are so busy being productive that we forget what it means to rest. But when practicing mindfulness, this is one of the most important aspects. In doing so, you can better equip yourself mentally—as well as physically—when it comes time to get back into the swing of things.

It might feel weird at first—especially if you have a long list of daily tasks that you're wanting to accomplish—but everyone needs a break, even if they think they don't. The reason behind this is because when you're continuously moving 24/7 this gives your brain—and body—very little time to recharge. With such a small window, you might eventually feel yourself experiencing burn-out, but the much-needed R&R (rest and relaxation) that stems from mindfulness can make all the difference.

Letting go of all that you're feeling in that current moment is also key. If you don't, you'll find that your practice in mindfulness will be extremely ineffective—when holding onto things like the past or looking too far ahead toward the future. In turn, releasing might be difficult at first but allows you to put your full focus on the task at hand.

In certain instances, you may feel as though you want to escape your current situation. But by letting go, you can live in the moment—and not just cope with how you're feeling. This is done through a mindful approach that repositions your thoughts on what is happening right now rather than on what might happen later. Also avoiding looking at your microwave, wall clock, or phone to check the time. Instead, just let go and be.

You may have heard the saying "think before you speak" while growing up, yet many of us frequently fail to follow suit. Even so—no matter how much you might struggle with this, mindfulness can help. When you begin to pay attention to not just your decisions but the reason behind each one, you'll find you can easily approach life with a whole new perspective. Only then can you become more mindful of not just how you treat others, but of how you treat yourself.

A judgment is much like a first impression, but how you view something initially can change within an instant. That's why it's important to be open-minded about your process as you go. However, mindfulness entails recognizing those judgments as they take place.

When starting out, make sure and prepare yourself for your mindful meditation by getting ready for the day—because how you feel can have a great influence on how you perform mentally. Just make sure that wherever you choose to practice is not only comfortable but quiet so that you're not easily disturbed.

Although it is most common to sit during meditation, you may choose to kneel or stand. Just make sure that whatever you pick is comfortable for you to remain in good posture. Ease yourself from any tension that you might feel by relaxing your body as a whole and focusing your mind on the task at hand. After all, you can only get out of your meditation what you put in, so rest your gaze and focus on your goals.

Your mind may begin to wander, but don't chastise yourself because of it—this is only natural. However, during the times that wandering takes place, forgive, forget, move forward, and focus on your breathing. This will help you regain focus entirely rather than wrestle with your thoughts. When you've finished your meditation, just remember that there is no need to rush and get up. Instead, it is most beneficial to bring yourself back to the reality that surrounds you.

Two examples of thoughts that people fixate on are their intentions and their work lives. These can begin to overwhelm and override the person's life, but fortunately, being in a state of mindfulness can relieve these types of thoughts, making for a happier life.

When using mindful meditation for anxiety, here are some things to remember.

Make sure that you aren't bent over so that the air you breathe is easily accessible to your lungs. Be sure that you're inhaling through your nose while meditating. This way, you will be able to breathe better and will avoid inhaling any pollutants that are in the air. Make sure that your breaths are deep and slow. In doing so, you will allow the air that you take in to go directly to your stomach, ensuring that you're breathing the correct way for the purposes of your meditation practice.

Shallow breathing is what you want to avoid, while deep breathing is what you want to embrace. In turn, make sure that each breath that you take is deep so that it can fill up your lungs entirely.

Mindfulness can offer you both strength and peace that you might not find otherwise. In doing so, you will no longer feel trapped by your mind, wishing for a way to cope, but can resume living a happy and healthy life—physically, mentally, and emotionally.

Boundary Defense

Preventative care is important, but what might be even more important is to train yourself to defend against those who are actively trying to undermine your emotional resilience and actually prefer you unstable. This is when you must proactively establish self-defense from others, whereas the rest of this book has been about defeating your own demons and defending against yourself. For our purposes, this comes in the form of defending your boundaries.

That people don't always behave as we'd like is a hard lesson to learn in all relationships. Seeing apathy, carelessness, or a lack of respect for others' feelings is a great source of stress and unhappiness. Trying to modify others to act and feel in ways we prefer is an exhausting and futile exercise.

All we *can* do is adjust ourselves and what we accept from others. We demonstrate our capacity for love, communication, support, and inspiration as best as we can and in ways we hope can be perceived. In others, we seek affirmation, or at least recognition, of our best efforts. In rare cases, we may find those whose ideals closely mirror our own. But ultimately, other people do what they're going to do, and we either accept them for who they are or walk away from them.

However, there's an element of relationships that you have more control over than you may think. It's a healthy kind of control that respects your values and feelings and reinforces your balanced relationships with others. That element is *setting and keeping emotional boundaries.*

This doesn't mean devising a list of ultimatums that other people must live up to, or risk losing your friendship. Neither does it mean erecting a wall around your emotions or feelings in over-protection. What boundaries *do* mean is making sure that you are caring for yourself first and foremost. They keep you happy, healthy, and emotionally balanced.

Boundaries in healthy relationships are strong and scrupled but flexible enough to respond to altered circumstances and each party's own uniqueness. They support each member's efforts to live full lives while developing legitimate respect, trust, and support over a long period of time. Setting up boundaries is an introspective and practical process, and occasionally, people will tell you that your boundaries are wrong. They might be right, but subjective boundaries also exist.

Define your limits. Be honest with yourself about the point where others' behavior crosses your personal lines for acceptance and safety. What subjects are you sensitive to, no matter how objectively silly they might sound? At what level does someone's voice go from concern to anger? What makes you comfortable, and what makes you anxious?

Monitor your feelings. "Trusting your gut" is certainly a key thing to do when you're confronted with an immediate situation. But pay close attention to how you're reacting in social or low-pressure circumstances as well. If a conversation's taking a turn that makes you uncomfortable, mark that point and ask yourself what could be causing your stress. Being self-aware in itself isn't a sign of narcissism or selfishness—it's a basic survival mechanism. Your annoyance, discomfort, or guilt is the red flag that your boundaries are being stomped on.

Set a communication plan. Very few of us talk or act the same way with every single person we know (if we do, that's probably a problem). But in close relationships, at some point the need to discuss our boundaries will arise, and you should make a plan in advance for how you will communicate your feelings. Being direct is always the preference, but the definition of our relationship is important in figuring out how to express that directness. In personal relationships, we might feel free to speak openly and ruminate. In professional or complicated situations, we may need to be level and determined.

Keeping up a sense of self-awareness, as mentioned, is a key part of relationship health. Being truthful about the effectiveness of our internal boundaries— and taking proactive, corrective measures when they fall short—is crucial to this honesty. It also goes a very long way in protecting one's self from the operations of emotional manipulators.

Even if we know and set our emotional boundaries, we may overlook them in practice with others or not always recognize when our boundaries are being trespassed. Since emotional manipulators thrive on blurring those boundaries and resetting them to reflect their own interests, developing a keener sense of when those trespasses happen is extremely useful.

It's easier to notice verbal violations, for obvious reasons. Any effort to invalidate or disparage you or your emotions should be evaluated in relation to your boundaries. These include someone not allowing you to speak or be heard by silencing or talking over you, screaming, making derogatory statements about your integrity, or even flat-out gossiping about you in plain sight. Violations of your psychological and emotional boundaries can be more difficult to spot and harder to quantify. They could include the following:

- preying on your self-esteem
- using things you've said to them in confidence against you
- lying
- criticizing, demeaning, and judging
- making fun of you or your thoughts, feelings, and beliefs
- making you feel guilty or responsible
- demanding your time and energy

- shaming and embarrassing
- bullying
- claiming their thoughts and beliefs are superior to yours

While defining and setting up boundaries is the important pivot point in any relationship, maintaining them is equally essential. Psychologist Dana Gionta identified two key feelings that should be red flags that we're letting go of our boundaries.

Discomfort. "When someone acts in a way that makes you feel uncontrollable, that's a cue to us they may be violating or crossing a boundary." Discomfort can arise from triggers about past issues or traumas, someone communicating in an overly frantic or antagonistic way, or being in an unexpected or unsafe situation. It can also simply arise from being put in a position where you feel interpersonal tension.

Resentment. This usually comes from being taken advantage of or not being appreciated. We feel that someone else is imposing their expectations on us. Resentment can arise when we're asked to fix an ongoing series of crises, when we get left out of important work decisions after habitually working overtime, or when we simply don't get anything back from what we give.

Gionta recommends gauging our feelings on a scale from one to ten and sounding the alarm if our intensity goes higher than six. When that happens, she suggests asking what's causing the feelings and what about the situation is bothering you.

Frequently, the root impetuses are fear, guilt, and self-doubt. We fear others' responses when we set and keep our boundaries. We feel guilty if we speak up or say no. And we doubt that we even deserve to have boundaries in the first place.

What we have to remember is that boundaries are key signs of a healthy relationship and vital steps toward self-respect. You're the exclusive owner of your own feelings, and as their protector, you have full permission to set and preserve your emotional boundaries. But knowing where you stand is a necessary measure in deciding your boundaries. Identify your limits: physical, emotional, mental, and spiritual. Concentrate on what you can tolerate and what you can't accept. "Those feelings help us identify what our limits are," Gionta says.

Take time to consider your present social circle and close friendships. Think about whether your give-and-take is healthy and whether the relationships are truly reciprocal. If you notice a certain behavioral strain or commonality with your friends (or with yourself), address it in your investigation, whether good or bad—it could help detect further clues about your emotional realities.

Finally, examine how your daily environment outside of relationships could be impacting your health. Your work environment is a good place to start. For example, if your workday is supposed to be eight hours but your coworkers regularly stay at least 10 or 11, is there an unspoken mandate that you're supposed to go "above and beyond"? How does your office cope with sudden emergencies or long-term conflicts?

Keeping boundaries intact is a solo exercise—it springs from your own personal observations and experience. It can be challenging, especially if somebody feels they're the only one trying to maintain boundaries. But it's a regular way to tend to our feelings and needs and a good mechanism to remind ourselves how we need to honor them.

Takeaways:

- What is preventative care in the context of mastering your emotions and keeping calm while the world spins on? It is recognizing the fact that our brains have an intense negativity bias, even while things are going well and we aren't on the brink of disaster. And thus, we should seek to immunize our resilience through daily actions.

- Be grateful. Savor everything. Enjoy the moment, because you'll never get it back. Both gratitude and savoring (slowing down and being intentional with your actions) have been scientifically shown to reduce stress and increase positivity and happiness. It's awfully tough to be both grateful and miserable at the same time. Proper perspective and expectations can be transformative for your emotional resilience.
- Journaling and writing your feelings down is not an uncommon piece of advice. It is the act of expressing yourself and then being able to introspect later on. Most of us miss these two important steps, and our emotions remain pent up and unable to develop and unfurl. Of particular use is writing down all of your worries and then writing down solutions for them. Also, you can write down two distinct types of lists: "Stop Doing This" (something detrimental) or "It's Okay To" (something beneficial).

- Mindfulness is a key part of preventative care. It is the release of stress from a past that doesn't matter anymore and a set of futures that may never come into existence. It is the act of letting go and feeling your emotions swirl around you, then observing them settle back into a normal place. It is the conscious ignorance of everything but one singular focus; this is a state of mind where no stress or anxiety can exist. You are peaceful; the more you practice, the more peace transfers into your daily life.
- Finally, we come to defense of your boundaries. This book has talked about how to deal with yourself—but what about others? After all, people are probably our strongest emotional triggers and they hold enormous power over us. The best step for this is to understand boundaries. Most of your negative spirals with others are related to boundaries, so we must see the warning signs, set boundaries, and enforce them. Any set of negative feelings probably means that your

boundaries are being violated in some way.

Summary Guide

Chapter 1. Our Volatile Emotions

- Our emotions have enormous power over us. Sometimes this is good, and other times, it makes us feel completely out of control. This is bad. But there is good reason for this type of power—you can view emotions as a type of warning signal that has evolved alongside humans to keep us alive and healthy. In the absence of higher critical thinking, emotions taught us about the world and how to regard it. This is also the reason that negative emotions can make us spiral out of control so quickly.
- These types of dangers aren't present anymore in our modern lives, and our task now is less survival and more controlling and harnessing our emotions. The extent to which we do this can wholly determine how our lives go. In no way is this suggesting that emotional suppression is the key to happiness. In fact, emotional

suppression is linked to poor health outcomes, so we must simply find the fine line of healthy emotional expression and reaction.

Chapter 2. Emotional Triggers

- When we talk about emotional resilience and calm, we are really talking about the emotional triggers that push us over the edge. The vast majority of the time, these triggers will be subtle and external and not at all proportionate (or even related) to the response they will create within you. This is the classic case of overreacting to a simple statement based on how it made you feel, not the actual substance.
- Of course, this is because our emotional needs are being exposed, poked, or prodded in an uncomfortable way. To escape this discomfort, we react by lashing out, avoiding, or coping in a variety of other ways. Very few of these habits are healthy, and this sequence of events is what will lead to your unraveling and emotional instability.

- It's not enough to simply know your emotional needs; we need to gain emotional granularity into what is actually happening. A doctor can only treat a sickness if they know the actual cause, and Plutchik's wheel of emotions is a useful tool in labeling yourself and escaping the uncertainty of a general feeling of dread and discomfort. In fact, diversity of emotion helps us remain balanced and even-keeled.

Chapter 3. Recognize, Respond, and Regulate

- Now that we've got an understanding of emotional triggers, needs, pain, and how they all interact with each other, we must talk about how to deal with them. How can we inject self-awareness into our lives, recognize what's happening, and keep the volcano (us) from erupting? The first model to think about is responding versus reacting. When we touch a hot stove, we are reacting without thought, instinctually, and to protect ourselves. This is rarely

necessary from an emotional standpoint, and yet we find ourselves similarly volatile to a volcano instead of pausing a beat to think and then respond.
- Next, we should think about a framework for regulation that plays with the emotional triggers and needs we have discussed. This consists of selecting the situation (avoiding triggers), modifying the situation (decreasing triggers), shifting focus (ignoring triggers), changing thoughts (changing the trigger), and changing response (reacting less to a trigger).
- This leads directly to the next point of distress tolerance. Sometimes we are indeed too prone to flying off the handle; we are overly sensitive in a way that makes us unpredictable and fragile. Thus, we need to work on increasing our tolerance to distress and anxiety. This has common elements with the framework for regulation, but it focuses more on foregoing the comforting escape mechanisms you use and staying in the situation and emotion. The purpose is to accept anxiety and

distress, withstand the major emotional spike surrounding it, and stay with it until it subsides and you realize that you are still doing fine.

Chapter 4. Cutting the Cycle

- Our lowest emotional points don't exist in isolation; they almost all exist due to various cycles of triggers, emotional needs, behaviors, and then consequences—all of which strengthen the cycle for the future. So it's necessary to cut the cycle short and interrupt it in any way that we can. The most valuable way we can do this is through simply analyzing how it takes place in our lives.

- The first tool for this is the ABC Loop, which stands for antecedent, behavior, and consequence. They generally describe the main elements of an emotional outburst that we can break down and analyze: what happens before, what you did to cope, and what happens afterward that makes the cycle even harder to escape.

- The second tool is similar but more in-depth: emotional dashboarding. It describes the same cycle but through a different lens, with elements of situations, thoughts, emotions, bodily sensations, and impulses/actions. This gives you an even deeper view into certain situations and why you felt the need to lash out or become dragged down by negativity. The important thing to keep in mind with both of these tools is that the willingness for deep honesty is required.

- Finally, we come to a tool that underlies everything: self-talk. Most of the time, our self-talk is negative and disempowering. We may not even realize that our lens on the world and ourselves is negative because we've held this type of narrative about our lives for so long. But negative self-talk just makes you less resilient. The world is neutral, and our self-talk is what determines our emotions much of the time. Self-awareness is the key here; would you speak to a close friend like you speak to yourself?

Chapter 5. The Emotional Immune System

- Self-esteem is the emotional immune system because it insulates you from emotional triggers, needs, and pains. The person who generally feels positively about themselves is not prone to emotional instability or reactivity because they simply aren't affected in the same way.
- Like the external world, our identities are entirely neutral, and self-esteem is a lens we view ourselves through. This means we have the power to see ourselves however we want, and for some of us, this is terrible news. A primary reason is an unreasonable set of expectations about yourself, the world, and your place in it—you will never live up to these expectations, so you can literally only fail in your mind, which makes you feel even worse than before.
- Self-esteem, as with many things about emotions, is not living in a vacuum and is best understood as a cycle of causes

and effects. We begin with inaccurate assumptions and arbitrary (and disempowering) rules about life that are confirmed through inevitable failure. Then our narrative begins to include this data point and creates an increasingly negative self-evaluation. The inaccurate assumptions and beliefs are then strengthened, and it becomes even more difficult to climb out of this pit of despair. Deciphering these beliefs and seeing them nullified by reality is key.

Chapter 6. Philosophical Perspective

- Sometimes a shift in perspective is all that is needed for something to finally click inside you. At the very least, we can combine these new perspectives with the techniques and tools we've learned to make you emotionally bulletproof.
- Here, we cover two of the world's oldest philosophies in dealing with hardship and optimizing for happiness. Buddhism is all about understanding that we cause our own suffering through attachment to people, things, outcomes, and thoughts. Everything is impermanent, and good

and bad come and go like waves on the ocean. When we form an attachment, we form an expectation, which puts us in a position to tumble and fall. Thus, we must detach from the notion that external things or people are necessary for our happiness. In this way, we make ourselves entirely responsible for our state of mind.

- Stoicism has some philosophical overlap with Buddhism, but the emphasis is on what we can and cannot control. We cannot control anything in this world but our actions and thoughts, so we must condition our happiness to depend happiness on those things. To do otherwise would be to remove all power from us. The world is a neutral place, and we can interpret it however we want; we only have to choose a favorable interpretation. In Stoicism, we must also turn the obstacle upside down and not see negative events as tragedy, but rather interpret and reframe them as learning experiences.

Chapter 7. Preventative Care

- What is preventative care in the context of mastering your emotions and keeping calm while the world spins on? It is recognizing the fact that our brains have an intense negativity bias, even while things are going well and we aren't on the brink of disaster. And thus, we should seek to immunize our resilience through daily actions.
- Be grateful. Savor everything. Enjoy the moment, because you'll never get it back. Both gratitude and savoring (slowing down and being intentional with your actions) have been scientifically shown to reduce stress and increase positivity and happiness. It's awfully tough to be both grateful and miserable at the same time. Proper perspective and expectations can be transformative for your emotional resilience.
- Journaling and writing your feelings down is not an uncommon piece of advice. It is the act of expressing yourself and then being able to introspect later on. Most of us miss these

two important steps, and our emotions remain pent up and unable to develop and unfurl. Of particular use is writing down all of your worries and then writing down solutions for them. Also, you can write down two distinct types of lists: "Stop Doing This" (something detrimental) or "It's Okay To" (something beneficial).
- Mindfulness is a key part of preventative care. It is the release of stress from a past that doesn't matter anymore and a set of futures that may never come into existence. It is the act of letting go and feeling your emotions swirl around you, then observing them settle back into a normal place. It is the conscious ignorance of everything but one singular focus; this is a state of mind where no stress or anxiety can exist. You are peaceful; the more you practice, the more peace transfers into your daily life.
- Finally, we come to defense of your boundaries. This book has talked about how to deal with yourself—but what about others? After all, people are probably our strongest emotional

triggers and they hold enormous power over us. The best step for this is to understand boundaries. Most of your negative spirals with others are related to boundaries, so we must see the warning signs, set boundaries, and enforce them. Any set of negative feelings probably means that your boundaries are being violated in some way.

Printed in Great Britain
by Amazon